Super Insulated Houses

and

Air-To-Air Heat Exchangers

Super Insulated Houses

and

Air-To-Air Heat Exchangers

William A. Shurcliff

BRICK HOUSE PUBLISHING COMPANY
Andover, Massachusetts

Library of Congress Cataloging-in-Publication Data

Shurcliff, William A.
 Superinsulated Houses and Air-to-Air Heat Exchangers / William
A. Shurcliff—Newly rev.
 p. cm.
 Combined rev. ed. of Super insulated houses, and Air-to-air heat
exchangers for houses.
 Includes bibliographies and indexes.
 ISBN 0-931790-73-5 (pbk.)
 1. Dwellings—Insulation. 2. Dwellings—Heating and
ventilation. 3. Heat exchangers. I. Shurcliff, William A. Super
insulated houses. II. Shurcliff, William A. Air-to-air heat exchangers for
houses. III. Title. IV. Title: Super insulated houses. V. Title: Air-to-
air heat exchangers.
TH1715.S519 1988   88-6987
693.8'32—dc19   CIP

Contents

Chapter 1
Preliminary Considerations

In about 1980 a whole new approach to fuel saving came to the attention of architects and builders. Called **superinsulation,** this approach provided a high degree of comfort in winter and summer, reduced fuel consumption by 75% to 95% relative to conventional houses, allowed the architect great flexibility of house design, and increased construction costs by only a few percent.

The method was announced and explained in talks at building construction conferences, in magazine articles, and in books. Enthusiasm spread rapidly, with the result that by 1987 there were several tens of thousands of superinsulated houses in routine use in the United States and Canada. The number of such houses has more than doubled each year. In some very cold regions, the new method now dominates home construction.

DEFINITION

Although there is no universally accepted definition of a superinsulated house, the following one is representative: a superinsulated house is one that receives only a modest amount of solar energy (for example, has a south-facing window area not exceeding 8% of the floor area), and is so well-insulated and so airtight that, throughout most of the winter, it is kept warm almost entirely by the modest amount of solar energy received through the windows and by intrinsic heat, that is, miscellaneous heat sources within the house. What little auxiliary heat is needed is less than 15% of that required by typical houses of comparable size built before 1974.

The 8% limit on south window area was chosen because, if the area is much greater, intake of solar energy may be more important than conserving heat from various internal sources. In other words, the house may be more a solar house than a superinsulated house, because large windows, even when double-glazed, lose large amounts of heat on cold nights.

Intrinsic Heat

By "miscellaneous heat sources within the house" is meant stoves for cooking, domestic hot water systems, human bodies, clothes washers, clothes dryers, dish washers, electric lights, television and radio sets, refrigerators, and other electric appliances.

Not included is heat from a furnace, electric heater, or living-room stove—or heat from solar radiation entering through windows.

Some writers like to think in terms of household intrinsic heat production *per person*. A typical value is 20,000 Btu per day per person.

From house to house there is, certainly, much variation in the total amount of intrinsic heat. Even in the same house, different families may have radically different intrinsic heat gain because of differences in appliances and in lifestyles. Also, over time a family's heat production can change considerably. A new baby or small child may greatly increase clothes washing, clothes drying, and hot water use, and thus directly increase intrinsic heat.

1

A house with efficient appliances used in a conserving manner may produce as little as 10,000 Btu per person per day if people are away at work or at school much of the day. Also, as lower power appliances come into use, the amounts of intrinsic heat produced become even smaller.

INTRINSIC HEAT

Source	Amount of intrinsic heat, in Btu, produced in a typical house in a typical 24-hour midwinter day
Human bodies (two adults, two children)	29,000
Cooking stove, microwave oven	18,600
Heater for domestic hot water	4,100
Clothes dryer	8,300
Miscellaneous electric equipment: clothes washer, dish washer, refrigerator, electric blankets, toaster, coffee pot, blowers, fans	59,500
Total	119,500

Auxiliary Heat

By "auxiliary heat" is meant heat from a system installed mainly for the purpose of space heating: for example, furnaces, space heaters or living-room heat stoves, all using oil, gas, electricity, coal, or wood.

The 15% comparative limit on auxiliary heat was chosen because a house that conforms to it can keep its occupants tolerably comfortable throughout a winter even if the auxiliary heat is cut off entirely. Typically, the house will never cool down to 32°F, so pipes will not freeze and thus never have to be drained, and faucets, sinks, toilets and tubs will continue to operate normally.

Furthermore, it would take only a little additional heat, as from a wood stove or one or two portable electric space heaters, to keep such a house comfortable.

HALLMARKS

The main distinguishing characteristics, or hallmarks, of a superinsulated house are:

- Thick and widely applied insulation. Even at the sills, headers, eaves, window frames, door frames, and electric outlet boxes at least a moderate amount of insulation is provided.
- Near-airtight construction, but with a steady and controlled supply of fresh air.
- Use of a vapor barrier (large plastic sheet or equivalent) to prevent moisture from migrating into cold regions within the walls, ceilings, etc.

- No very large south-facing window area and even smaller areas facing west, north, east.
- No large furnace or heating system. There may be a small direct-vent gas heater or electric heater or a wood-burning stove, but it is used only rarely.
- No large system for distributing heat among the rooms.

There is, of course, no single best set of values of insulation thickness, window areas, etc. The designer must take into account the particular climate of the house-site chosen. A design that is optimum for Boston will not be optimum for sunny Colorado, cloudy Rochester, or bitterly cold Anchorage.

The above-listed hallmarks, or special strategies, are discussed in detail in later chapters.

BENEFITS

Superinsulation provides a rich harvest of benefits:

A superinsulated house remains at a steady and comfortable temperature throughout the winter, on sunny days and also on cold overcast days. Occupants benefit from the absence of drafts, cold floors, and cold spots near windows. The house tends to stay fairly cool in summer, especially if windows are kept closed during the hottest part of the day and are opened during the cool night. Little air-conditioning—perhaps none at all—is needed.

Little auxiliary heat is needed, and, thanks to the "smoothing" action of the excellent insulation, an especially small (and simple and safe) auxiliary heating system suffices. The cost of auxiliary heat is remarkably low—almost negligible compared to various other household expenses. Solar radiation plays an important role in heating the house, but the south window area is small enough that serious overheating on warm, sunny days is avoided.

Usually a forced supply of fresh air is provided, and the heat in the outgoing stale air is recovered by means of an air-to-air heat exchanger. The humidity of room air tends to remain comfortably high. The usual excessive dryness of indoor air in winter is avoided. The air-to-air heat exchanger prevents the humidity from rising too high.

Because main reliance is on heat conservation (excellent insulation, excellent retention of intrinsic heat) rather than on solar radiation, the superinsulated house is tolerant of less-favorable sites and orientations. It is permissible to locate such a house in a moderately wooded area and to employ a far from south-facing direction (orientation). Also, a great variety of design types are acceptable; the house does not have to appear strange and does not have to conform to a special style.

COST

The extra cost of superinsulating the house is only a few percent of the cost of the house as a whole: 3 to 6% typically. The added costs of extra insulation, vapor barrier, and air-to-air heat exchanger are partly offset by *not* having an expensive furnace, chimney, heat-distribution system, and large air-conditioning system.

ORIGINS OF SUPERINSULATION

Although superinsulation has become widely known only in the last five years, first efforts in this direction began more than forty years ago. Some of the early work is summarized below.

Small Homes Council: the Lo-Cal Design

In America one of the first groups to undertake large scale exploration, development, and promotion of the superinsulated house was the Small Homes Council of the University of Illinois. Its efforts culminated in the design of the Lo-Cal House.

The design was developed by a faculty team of architects and engineers at the university. Prominent on the team were Professors Warren S. Harris, Rudard A. Jones, Wayne L. Shick, and Seichi Konzo. In the 1940s this group began analyzing heat losses from houses, and by the early 1970s it had completed laboratory tests and calculations that clearly demonstrated the effectiveness of thick insulation, airtightness, and placing most of the windows on the south side of the house. They then created a detailed design that included all the features needed.

In 1976, with the aid of computers, the group proved that its proposed Lo-Cal House situated in a cold location would need only one third as much auxiliary heat as the designs then being promoted by HUD (U.S. Department of Housing and Urban Development).

The Lo-Cal house is actually a set of four carefully worked out conceptual designs suited to different sites and orientations but all using similar features and stressing superinsulation. Type A, a single-story house, is the basic design. The next most important design is Type D, a two-story house.

The Small Homes Council built many experimental houses, but never built a house exactly according to the Lo-Cal design. Many architects and builders in the United States and Canada have built homes that conform closely to the design. It has been estimated that since the detailed plans were published, several thousand houses of Lo-Cal type have been built.

Other Pioneers

The Illinois group's ideas greatly influenced the Canadian group that was designing the Saskatchewan Conservation House, which when constructed was found to need practically no auxiliary heat. This house, completed in 1978, is described in Chapter 3. The Illinois group's ideas were put to use also by Eugene Leger when he was planning his East Pepperell MA house; when it was completed in 1979 it was found to require less than $50 worth of gas heat per year. Details are presented in Chapter 4.

Meanwhile, working independently near Tupper Lake NY, R. P. Bentley built a superinsulated house employing a special stressed-skin (built-up beam) type of exterior wall. His design proved to be successful. (It is described in his 1975 book *Thermal Efficiency Construction*, published from Box 786-T, Tupper Lake NY 12986.)

In this same period Edward McGrath, in Alaska, tried out schemes employing drastically improved insulation in walls and roof and employing vapor barriers to prevent moisture from accumulating within walls and ceilings. In Alaska's harsh climate his designs were outstandingly successful. (They are described in his 1978 book *How to Build a Superinsulated House*, published by Project 2020, Box 80707, College AK 99708). This book is still good reading.

Many of the ideas presented in McGrath's book included contributions by a fellow Alaskan Axel Carlson, then working at Cooperative Extension, University of Alaska. (Reports on design details worked out by him are included in reports published by Cooperative Extension, University of Alaska, Fairbanks AK 99701.) Carlson later retired, and his work was continued by Richard Seifert.

A moderate degree of superinsulation was embodied in designs worked out in Arkansas by L. Blades of the Arkansas Power and Light Company. In the 1960s Blades, assisted by H. Tschumi, was looking for ways of reducing building heat losses in order to facilitate the use of heat pumps. The first energy crisis added to the sense of urgency, and F. Holtzclaw of HUD arranged the funding of construction of 35 well-insulated demonstration houses in various climates. Performance was found to be good and the designs were widely publicized. (Later designs, developed elsewhere in later years, have partially superseded the Arkansas designs.)

In 1979 the Mid-American Solar Energy Complex, a Minnesota group, promoted a broad family of single-family house designs employing such a favorable combination of insulation, window areas, and window locations (mostly south locations) that the amount of auxiliary heat needed in winter is very small. The group established a specific criterion, or upper limit, on the amount of auxiliary heat needed: the *Solar 80 Criterion*. Before succumbing to federal budget cutting in 1982, MASEC helped publicize superinsulation with reports, publications, and talks to builders.

In August of 1980 a big boost was given to superinsulation by a prestigious "brain-trust" group at the University of California. This government-supported group, led by A. H. Rosenfeld of the Lawrence Berkeley Laboratory and charged with exploring a wide variety of energy-saving strategies, took a hard look at superinsulation. It employed sophisticated theories to predict which energy-saving features would be effective, then examined existing superinsulated houses in some detail. It issued impressive reports giving full endorsement to superinsulation. Both theory and practice proved, the reports showed, that superinsulation is highly successfully technically and is cost-effective. The group also contributed to ideas as to fresh-air requirements in superinsulated houses and the effectiveness of air-to-air heat exchangers for capturing heat from outgoing stale air.

Newer Programs

By 1987 the enthusiasm for superinsulation had spread across the United States and Canada. Hundreds of builders were hard at work building superinsulated houses. Thousands of builders and architects flocked to seminars and training sessions arranged by Canadian government agencies and by private groups in the US. Many new building programs were launched.

In Washington state the Bonneville Power Administration launched a major demonstration project. More than 200 superinsulated houses were built and hundreds more were planned. Some homes of mobile type were included. Accurate cost-accounting methods were worked out. One conclusion, applicable to houses in four contiguous states, was that the installation of a vapor barrier adds $500 to $1,000 to the costs of the house. Also, the incremental cost of a vapor barrier, added insulation, and air-to-air heat exchanger amounted to about $3 per sq ft of floor area, or about $3,000 to $5,000 per house. The project including monitoring of indoor air; no significant problems were found.

In Minnesota in 1980, the Minnesota Home Finance Agency managed a superinsulation-and-solar program. Twenty-three builders participated and more than 100 houses were built. Performance studies showed that better results were achieved with superinsulation (less auxiliary heat needed, greater comfort, lower overall cost) than with standard solar houses.

In South Dakota, in 1985 and 1986, more than 50 superinsulated houses were built. Floor areas ranged from 1,100 to 3,800 sq ft, and typical annual heating costs ranged from $150 to $300. (Documented in the booklet *South Dakota Energy-Efficient Homes for the 80s,* available free from South Dakota Energy Office, 217-1/2 W. Missouri St., Pierre SD 57501).

Early in 1987 the Alaska state government took a hand in promoting superinsulation. It created an Alaska Craftsman Home program, patterned on the Canadian R-2000 program, that promoted superinsulation in many forceful ways. (Details are available from Cooperative Extension Service, Suite 240, 2221 E. Northern Lights Blvd., Anchorage AK 99508.)

Canada's Big Push

In 1984 the federal government of Canada, acting through its Department of Energy, Mines and Resources, launched a massive R-2000 Super Energy Efficient Home Program (also called Building Energy Technology Transfer, or BETT) designed to encourage builders and the buying public to embrace superinsulation. Backed by $100 million in funding, this program

- encouraged improvements in superinsulation techniques,
- established standards of excellence of superinsulation, general air-tightness, and prevention of flow of moisture into cold within-wall regions,
- ran two-day free training sessions on superinsulation techniques,
- offered free technical review and expected-performance evaluations of builders' proposed designs,
- provided a certification service for buildings meeting the standards,
- gave a $5,000 award to each builder on completion of his first house meeting the standards and a $1,500 award on completion of the second such house,
- gave great publicity, through newspapers, radio, and television, to the merits of superinsulation.

The builder was required to:

- have a technical representative attend an official training session,
- submit a proposed design (before start of construction) for evaluation and approval,
- permit extensive monitoring of the thermal performance of the house,
- allow visitors to inspect the house during certain hours each week, for one month.

Prospective house buyers benefited from having an authoritative certification that the house was well-insulated and tightly built and that the annual heating bills would be very low. Builders benefited from receiving free instruction and advice and from receiving a certificate that had great appeal to buyers. The R-2000 program enjoyed broad assistance from industry, from private institutions such as the Heating, Refrigerating, and Air Conditioning Institute of Canada, and also from various home builders' associations. Progress has been especially rapid in Saskatchewan, where four powerful groups have joined forces: the federal government, the provincial government, university technical schools, and the building industry. Today, in some parts of Saskatchewan, virtually every newly constructed home employs superinsulation.

Chapter 2
Lo-Cal House

In this and the following two chapters we present detailed descriptions of three historic superinsulated houses: the University of Illinois Lo-Cal House, the Leger House, and the Saskatchewan Conservation House. In a later chapter we discuss retrofitting existing houses, that is, drastically upgrading their insulation and airtightness.

Throughout, we give much attention to insulation, windows, vapor barriers, air change, and thermal performance generally. Little attention is given to finishes, beauty, and general architectural merit: these are important, but are outside the scope of this book.

None of the three historic houses discussed here has a conventional furnace. None requires a substantial amount of auxiliary heat. In a mild winter with the house well managed and a room temperature slightly below 70°F, almost no auxiliary heat may be needed. In a cold winter, with the house imperfectly managed a temperature of 70°F demanded at all times, an amount of auxiliary heat equivalent to that produced by 100 to 200 gallons of oil may be needed.

In other words, the amount of auxiliary heat needed is so small that it is almost "within the noise," that is, so small as to be hard to predict, hard to measure. Depending on many details of weather, house management, and occupants' style of living, it may be anywhere from zero to 20 million Btu (the heat produced by about 200 gallons of oil).

Lo-Cal House, Type A

This house, designed by bold experts at the Small Homes Council of the University of Illinois in the mid 1970s, was proposed for use in climates such as that of Madison, Wisconsin, a very cold city. Its winter coldness is specified by a degree-day value of 7,550.

What does **degree-day** mean? Consider a winter's day in which the average temperature is 35°F. Subtract this from the "standard nominal indoor temperature" of 65°F. The difference, 30 degrees, is the degree-day value—the coldness—of that day. Make this same calculation for all days of winter, add them up, and the total is then the annual degree-day value for the location in question. For Madison WI the total is 7,550.

The design is somewhat flexible. It can be modified to suit a wide range of climates: a degree-day range as large as 4,500 to 8,000. Major components of the design are discussed individually below.

Building as a whole. The Type A Lo-Cal House includes one story, 1,570 sq ft of floor area (56 ft x 28 ft), three bedrooms, attic space (cold), crawl space (moderately cold), and an attached two-car garage. It employs wood frame construction. The house faces exactly south. The effective thermal mass of house and furniture is 30,000 lb.

The living room and three bedrooms are on the south side and the kitchen-dining room, entrances, utility room, and two bathrooms are on the north side. There are two entrances, each of air-lock (vestibule) type; one includes a coat closet; the other, which is larger, serves as a utility room. When the sun heats the living room, hot air from the room circulates freely into the kitchen-dining room via an 8-ft-wide floor-to-ceiling opening.

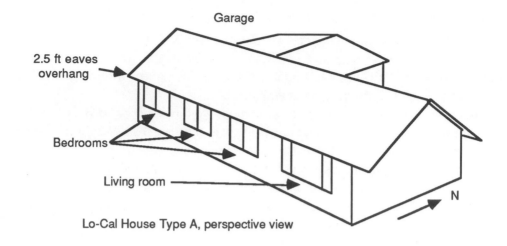

Lo-Cal House Type A, perspective view

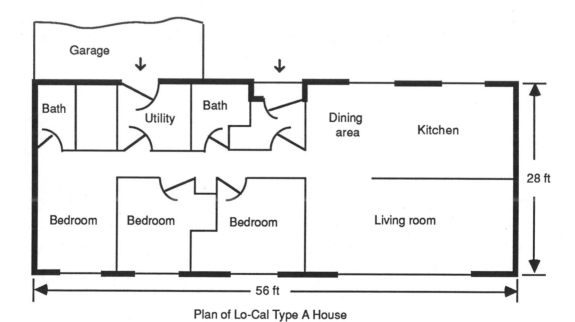

Plan of Lo-Cal Type A House

Windows. The total window area is 144 sq ft. Of this, 85 percent (122 sq ft) is on the south side and the remainder (22 sq ft) is on the north side. There are no windows on the east or west sides. Note that the area of the south-facing windows is about 8% of the gross floor area. All windows are triple glazed. The windows are equipped with privacy shades but no thermal shades or shutters.

Walls. Each wall as a whole, that is, each wall system, includes an outer wall and an inner wall, each employing 2x4 studs with centers 24 in. apart. One set of studs is offset 12 in. from the other, so that there is no through-stud path for heat flow. A 1.5-in. space between the two walls allows wiring to be run without drilling holes in the studs. The inner wall spaces, outer wall spaces, and between-walls space are filled with fiberglass batts that have no vapor barrier. The fiberglass is installed in two stages: first, R-11 or R-13 batts are installed in the outer wall. After the wiring is in place, R-19 batts are installed in the space between walls and in the inner wall space (a combined space 5 in. thick).

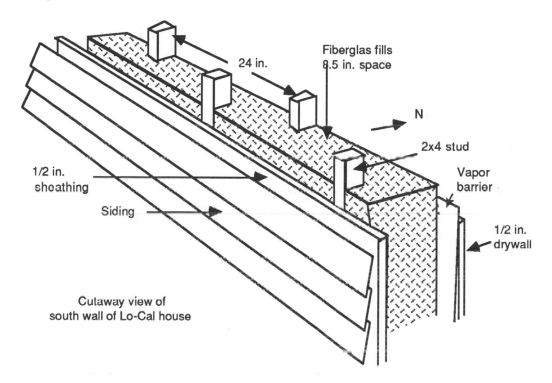

Cutaway view of
south wall of Lo-Cal house

The vapor barrier, a sheet of 0.006-in.-thick (6 mil) polyethylene, is installed on the room side of the inner wall, separated from the room space only by the half-inch-thick drywall. If some moisture should somehow penetrate into the wall system, this moisture would migrate upward in the 1.5-in. space between the inner and outer walls and pass into the attic, and from here it would pass to the outdoor via attic vents. (The blocking between the top plates of inner and outer walls is intermittent, to allow moisture to escape into the attic.)

On the outside of the outer wall is a half-inch sheathing of fiberboard, faced with wood clapboard siding.

The thickness of the wall before drywall or sheathing is installed is 8.5 in. The thickness including drywall and sheathing is 9.5 in. Overall thickness, including siding, is about 11 in. The nominal thermal resistance of the complete wall is R-33.

Sills. Fiberglass insulation extends downward to the sills and joins with the top of the subfloor insulation.

Floor. The floor includes a vapor barrier and, lower down, a 5.5-in. layer of fiberglass. Beneath some areas of the floor are water pipes situated beneath the vapor barrier but above the fiberglass. The resistance of the fiberglass is R-19. This R-19 insulation also fully covers the band-joist perimeter of the floor system.

Fixed frames of windows and doors. Even here there is considerable insulation. There is a 5.5-in. layer of fiberglass except at plates and studs, where there is only 1.5 in. A half-inch plate of Thermax (R-4) is used as a filler between the two 2x6 or 2x8 headers unless the headers are nail-and-glued plywood headers which have space for fiberglass insulation.

Ceiling. Within the ceiling proper is a vapor barrier, and above the ceiling proper there are 12 in. of fiberglass (R-38). The ceiling as a whole provides R-39 to R-41.

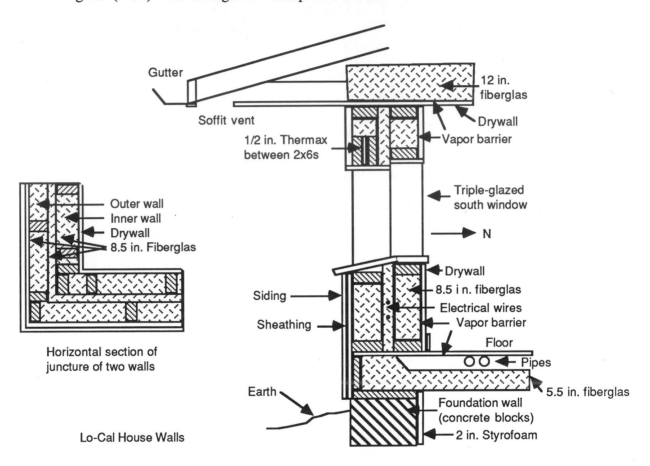

Horizontal section of juncture of two walls

Lo-Cal House Walls

Vertical section of south wall

Eaves. The eaves proper extend 26 in. outward from the outer face of the wall, and the horizontal underside (soffit) is at the same height as the ceiling proper. Accordingly, there is some free attic space directly above the wall, enough space so that the 12-in. layer of fiberglass can extend outward to cover completely the top of the wall system.

Vents. Vents extend along the full lengths of the soffits and the ridge of the roof.

Foundation wall. Each foundation wall is insulated on the inner side with 2 in. of Styrofoam (R-10). The overall resistance of the above-grade portion of the wall is then R-13. Below grade, where the earth helps, the overall resistance is much greater. For the wall as a whole, the effective resistance about R-20.

Caulking. Great care must be taken to caulk all remaining cracks.

Air change. Assumed to be typical is 0.5 air changes per hour. To keep the rate this high may require slight opening of windows or occasional use of forced air change via an air-to-air heat-exchanger. When there is no ventilation the rate may be as low as 0.2 changes per hour, which under some circumstances is not sufficient.

Humidity. No humidity problem is likely to exist, because exhaust fans in kitchen and bathroom vent moisture to the outdoors. In any event not much moisture condenses on triple-glazed windows.

Auxiliary heat. Electric.

Domestic hot water heating. Electric, preferably with solar preheating.

Solar heating. Much solar energy is collected via the south windows. Because they are triple-glazed, they gain more energy during daylight hours of a typical day in winter than they lose during 24 hours. During the heating season, a typical square foot of the triple-glazed south window produces a net gain of about 200 to 400 Btu per typical 24-hour day, the exact amount depending of the latitude, weather conditions, etc. In regions that have especially sunny and mild winters and much snow cover, the net gain is much greater.

Shading by eaves and gutters. The eaves project 26 in. from the outer face of the south wall, and eaves and gutters together project 30 in. The tops of the south windows are 16 in. lower than the eaves, and the window height is 50 in. If the house is at 43 degrees N, these windows are about 90% exposed to direct radiation from October 21 to February 21 and less than 20% from April 21 to August 21.

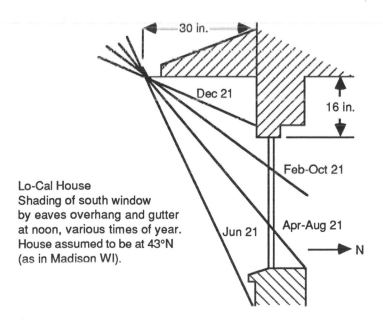

Lo-Cal House
Shading of south window
by eaves overhang and gutter
at noon, various times of year.
House assumed to be at 43°N
(as in Madison WI).

Cooling in summer. A total air-conditioning capacity of 8,000 Btu/hr is sufficient at nearly all times. If there are only two or three persons in the house, there may be no need for air conditioning.

Construction costs. Believed to be only a few percent more than that of the HUD 1974 house. The cost of the added insulation, etc., is largely offset by the saving from having no furnace and a simpler heat distribution system and the saving from using a smaller air conditioning system.

Performance. Computer calculations indicated that the greatest amount of heat that would be required from the auxiliary heating system of such a house situated in Madison, Wisconsin, would be 16,500 Btu per hour, or 396,000 Btu per day. Assuming certain severe conditions (the so-called design heat loss), we arrive at the breakdown of heat losses for this house and for the HUD 1974 House—which HUD innocently regarded, in 1974, as a highly energy efficient house—shown in the following tables.

COMPARATIVE HEAT-LOSS RATES

Component responsible for heat loss	Component area (sq ft)	Heat-loss rate (Btu/hr) on extremely cold day Loc-Cal House	HUD 1974 House
Ceiling	1,568	2,980	5,960
Walls	1,160	2,670	6,960
Floor	1,568	1,570	3,140
Windows	144	4,000	7,020
Door	40	200	200
Air change at 0.5 per hour		8,470	8,470
Totals		19,890	31,750

COMPARATIVE ANNUAL HEAT GAINS

Source of gain	Annual gain (Btu) Low-Cal House	HUD 1974 House
Intrinsic sources	13.1 million	13.1 million
From solar radiation	14.3 million	10.8 million
From auxiliary heater	13.0 million	38.0 million
Totals	40.4 million	61.9 million

The amount of auxiliary heat required per winter for the Lo-Cal house (13 million Btu) could be provided by burning about 130 gallons of fuel oil.

The HUD 1974 house would use about three times as much oil, and typical houses of comparable size and shape could use five times as much.

The modest amount of cooling required in summer in the Lo-Cal house would require only about 500 kWh of electricity (to operate conventional air conditioners), assuming that windows are opened on cool nights.

Design improvements and variations. Possible improvements include adjustable eaves overhang, thermal shutters for windows, and reduction of air change rate to 0.2 per hour when circumstances are favorable.

Possible variations include replacing clapboard siding with brick veneer; replacing sheathing and siding with 5/8-in. plywood; using a wood or coal burning stove instead of electrical heaters; using another kind of (e.g., solar) heat for domestic hot water; installing one or two very small windows on the east and west sides; using a larger area of south windows if the climate is especially sunny in winter; increasing attic insulation to 18 in. (R-60); increasing the space between walls to 3.5 in. to allow room for two more inches of insulation, to total 10.5 in. (R-40); and providing an air-to-air heat exchanger.

Lo-Cal House, Type D

The type-D house is the next most important design developed by the Illinois group. It has two stories. Being compact, it is suitable for small lots. Thus, it is applicable to townhouses.

The general features are much like those of the type-A house. Possible improvements include installing a second-story balcony to shade first-story windows in summer.

Chapter 3
Leger House

The Leger House is located in East Pepperell, Massachusetts (35 miles northwest of Boston), 42.5 degrees N, 7,000 degree days. The designer and builder was Eugene H. Leger, now living in New Ipswich NH.

It is a one-story, 46 ft by 26 ft, ranch-style wood-frame house with a floor area of 1,200 sq ft, a full basement, and a small attic space. There is no garage. The main story includes a kitchen and dining room, living room, three bedrooms, a bathroom, and two outside entrances. The unheated attic is 5 ft high at the center and is reached by a ceiling access panel in the west vestibule. The house faces 20 degrees east of south.

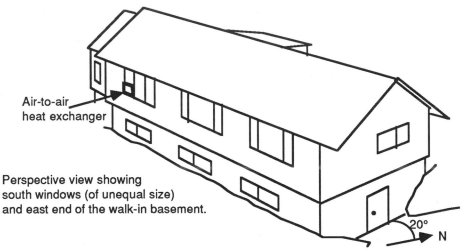

Air-to-air heat exchanger

Perspective view showing south windows (of unequal size) and east end of the walk-in basement.

20° N

COMPONENTS

Windows and doors. The entrances are of airlock vestibule type. The total window area is 153 sq ft, of which two thirds is on the south side. All of the windows have wood frames. About 70% of the window area is triple glazed, and the remainder is doubled glazed. There are privacy shades but no thermal shades.

Above the windows and doors are box beams, hollow structures built on site that provide much strength but, when filled with cellulose fiber, conduct very little heat. Each box beam, made of 2x4 stringers and stiffeners and half-inch plywood facing sheet or webs, is about 4.5 inches thick. Above each window or door two box beams are used, to provide an overall thickness of 9 inches.

Heat loss through the fixed frames around the windows and doors was kept small by caulking all cracks with urethane foam.

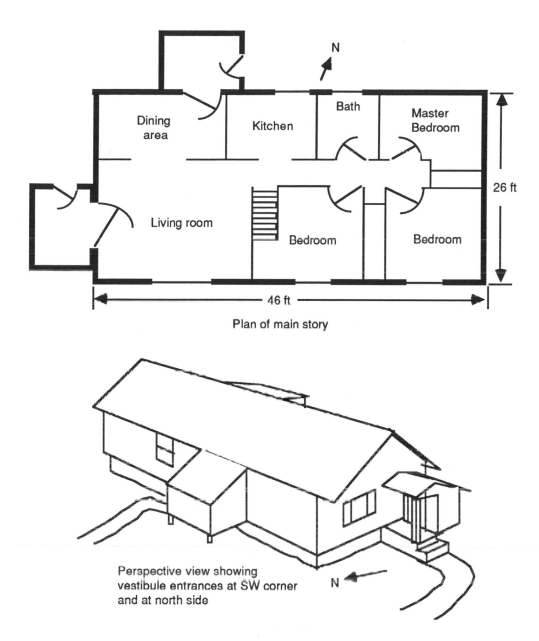

Plan of main story

Perspective view showing
vestibule entrances at SW corner
and at north side

Walls. There is an outer wall and an inner wall, each employing 2x4 studs 24 in. apart on centers. One set of studs is offset 12 in. relative to the other so that there is no path for heat flow within the studs all the way through. There is a 2-in. space between the walls. This space, together with the two sets of spaces between the studs, is filled with cellulose fiber. On the room side of the inner wall there is a vapor barrier of 5-mil polyethylene and two layers of half-inch gypsum board. On the outside of the outer wall there is a sheathing of 1-in. tongue-and groove Styrofoam covered by the siding, which consists of vinyl sheets formed to resemble clapboards.

The overall thickness of the wall is 12 in. Before the siding, sheathing, and gypsum boards were installed, the thickness was 9 in.

The cellulose fiber was installed in the wall system in two stages. The first stage was completed before the vapor barrier and gypsum boards were installed. The second stage was done after the vapor barrier and one layer of gypsum board were installed: holes were drilled through the gypsum board and vapor barrier, and the cellulose fiber was blown in. The holes were then filled with wooden plugs and sealed with taped-on pieces of polyethylene film. The second layer of gypsum board was then installed.

The thermal resistance of the 9 in. of cellulose fiber is about R-36, and the resistance of the complete 12-in.-thick wall is about R-43.

There are no holes through the outer or inner walls. None were necessary, because the pertinent electric wires were installed on the room face of the wall system; specifically, a continuous 3-wire flat vinyl strip was applied as a horizontal band to the room side of the inner wall.

Electrical outlet boxes were connected to the strip at appropriate locations. The strip was painted in wall-matching color so as to be inconspicuous. (The wires could, of course, have been installed conveniently in the space between the inner and outer sets of studs). Also, there are no pipes in the wall system.

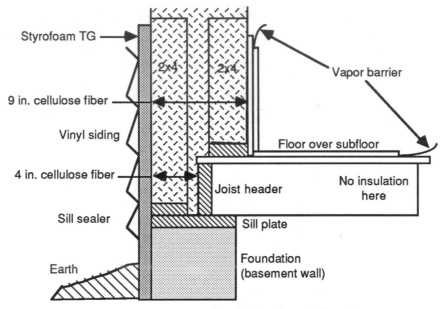

Vertical section of sill region

Sills. These are well insulated by 4 in. of cellulose fiber and 1 in. of tongue-and-groove Styrofoam outside the joist header.

Roof support. The roof is supported by prefabricated trusses, the load being borne by the external walls. The partition walls carry no load.

Attic. There are 10 in. of blown cellulose fiber resting on the floor of the attic. Just beneath the insulation there is the vapor barrier; no wires pass through it and there is only one hole through it, for the bathroom vent pipe. This vapor barrier overlaps, and is sealed to, the vapor barrier serving the walls. There are full-length soffit vents and a full-length ridge vent.

Floor. Oak flooring is laid on a 6-mil poly vapor barrier, which in turn rests on plywood subflooring. Note: the floor was installed before any partitions were erected; thus it comprises one large rectangular area with no interruptions. The partitions rest on the finished oak floor, and could easily be relocated or removed if desired.

Basement. The full basement has a walkout at the east end. The walls are of 10-in.-thick poured concrete. The south, west, and north walls are insulated externally, from top to bottom, with 1-in. tongue and groove Styrofoam. The east wall is partially insulated. The door in that wall is of insulation-filled steel. There are three small basement windows on the south side with fixed vinyl frames and double glazing (of Plexiglas).

Vapor barrier. Vapor barriers of 5-mil or 6-mil polyethylene are used on all four wall systems of the main story and on the ceiling and floor. All vapor barriers are overlapped and sealed at the overlaps.

Humidity. At most times during the winter the relative humidity remains between 50% and 60%, which makes conditions very comfortable. On a few occasions the humidity reaches 70% but may be reduced by opening windows or turning on a small dehumidifier of conventional type. During most of the summer, with windows and doors open for long periods, humidity is usually below 60%. Sometimes it is higher and may be reduced by turning on a 20-in.-diameter exhaust fan (with windows or doors open).

Air change. When pressurized to 50 pascals (0.2-in. water), said to equal the infiltration capacity of a 25-30 mph wind, the house has an air-leakage rate corresponding to 2.5 air changes per hour, according to tests. (Earlier, with some cracks not yet sealed, the rate was almost twice as great.) No data are available as to the air-change rate under typical conditions of wind speed and direction; however, it is estimated by the builder that the rate is a small fraction of one change per hour.

Exchanger. Early in 1980 a Mitsubishi Lossnay Model VL-155, 56-watt, air-to-air heat exchanger, delivering 65 cfm at 70% efficiency, was installed at the west end of the southwest window.

Auxiliary heat. A small (knapsack-size) Paloma Constant-Flo gas heater, Model PH-6, serves a separate 40-gal tank that has 6 in. of insulation. The heater weighs 20 lb, is rated at 43,800 Btu/hr, and provides 1.4 gpm of water with 50°F degrees of temperature rise. Domestic hot water is heated by a heat exchanger in the tank. The hot water in the tank loops directly through a 40-ft baseboard radiator, to provide auxiliary room heat. During the first four months of 1979, the total amount of auxiliary heat used was 11 million Btu. The combustion products of the heater are discharged to the outdoors through a horizontal 2-ft-long pipe, 3 in. in diameter. A small blower in this pipe speeds the discharge; the blower runs whenever the heater runs. The cost of installing a chimney was saved.

Summer cooling. A small conventional air conditioner was installed and was used in summer for 10 or 20 hours in all. On most hot summer days the rooms remain satisfactorily cool (80°F or below) if doors and windows are kept shut and shades drawn. A 20-in. electric fan is sometimes operated to cool the house at night—a slow process. In periods of hot nights, running the air conditioner briefly is necessary to keep the house cool.

Costs. The house cost about 2% more to build than a conventional house of similar size, not counting the considerable labor of the designer-builder. The many special heat-saving features added about $2,000, and the compensating savings from having no furnace or chimney and a smaller heat distribution system were about $1,500. The net incremental cost is impossible to compute accurately, but obviously was reasonably small.

Possible improvements. Provide adjustable eaves or shades to cut down solar radiation in autumn. Reduce the south window area about 20%.

Chapter 4

Saskatchewan Conservation House

In the mid-1970s a team of Canadian architects, engineers, and physicists began the design of a house destined to delight and astonish energy conservationists throughout North America. Located in one of the coldest cities of the continent (Regina, in Saskatchewan; a 10,800 degree-day location), this house was to remain warm with practically no auxiliary heat. No oil, gas, or wood heating system was provided. If heat was required, the requirement could be met by turning on one or two burners of the electric cooking stove.

The design team included experts from the Canadian Federal Department of Mineral Resources, from several agencies of the Saskatchewan provincial government, the two major Saskatchewan colleges of engineering, and several other forward-looking institutions. David Eyre was Project Manager, and Hendrik Grolle was the architect.

In an excess of ambition and daring, the group overdesigned the building. It had more energy-saving and solar-energy-collecting features than were needed. Some unnecessary complexities were introduced, and costs were excessive. Yet the project was overwhelmingly successful and convinced thousands of architects and builders that superinsulation held the key to comfort and low-cost heating.

HOUSE AS A WHOLE

The Saskatchewan Conservation house is a two-story wood frame house oriented 21 degrees west of south. It has outside dimensions of 44x26 ft, inside dimensions of 42x24 ft, and a total floor are of 2,016 sq ft. There is a crawl space, but no basement and no garage. The house has a passive solar heating system and a water-type active solar system that mainly serves to heat domestic hot water but can supply space heating also. There is no large thermal mass in the walls or floors.

The first story includes the family room, living room, kitchen-dining room, bathroom, and two vestibule airlock outside entrances at the southwest and northeast corners. The second story includes three bedrooms, a bathroom, den, and laundry. In the northwest corner of the house there is a steel two-story-high tank for storing hot water. On the south face of the attic there is a solar collector.

The main roof area slopes 70 degrees upward to the north. The eaves extend 4 ft south from the peak of the roof, and a fin-like catwalk just above the second story windows extends 2 ft.

COMPONENTS

Attic, floors and doors. The attic floor is covered with 16 in. of cellulose fiber (R-60). In the first-story floor, 9.5 in. of cellulose fiber (R-36) was installed between the 2x10 floor joists.

The external doors in the airlock vestibules are steel clad and contain 1.75 in. of urethane. At the edges are wooden thermal breaks.

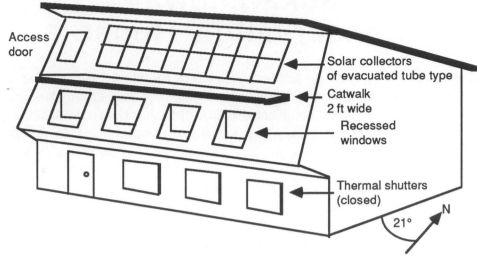

Building support. The building rests on 19 concrete pilings and on 8-in.-thick concrete grade beams insulated on the side toward the building interior with 6 in. of extruded polystyrene foam (R-30). On the outside, 12 in. below the surface of the ground, is a horizontal apron of extruded polystyrene foam.

Vapor barrier. In the external walls, foundation walls, first-story floor, and second-story ceiling, vapor barriers of 6-mil polyethylene are installed. In each case the sheet is situated on the warm or inner side of the insulation. Great care was taken to maintain the integrity of the barriers; overlaps and seals were used; perforations were kept to a minimum and sealed. Molded bags of polyethylene were installed at each electrical outlet box and were sealed to the vapor barrier.

Walls. Each exterior wall has two separate frames. The outer one employs 2x4s, and the inner one employs either 2x4s or 2x6s, the latter being used on the first story. Within each frame the studs are 24 in. apart on centers. The two sets of studs are aligned, not offset 12 in.

Each wall includes 13 in. of fiberglass. This is made up of three layers: two 3.5-in. batts and one 5.5-in. batt. The overall resistance is about R-44. On the warm side of the insulation there is a 6-mil poly sheet.

Windows. The total window area is 148 sq ft. Of this 128 sq ft or 87% is on the south side, and 20 sq ft or 13% is on the north.

There are no windows on the east or west sides. Half the window area is triple glazed and half is double glazed.

The area of the south windows is 6.4% of the floor area of the heated living space.

All windows are covered at night by thick, tightly sealed shutters. The shutters for the first-story south windows are 6 ft x 4 ft x 4 in., are Styrofoam-filled, and provide R-20. The edge seals are of rubber tubes. These shutters are hinged at the top and can be swung outward and upward by means of electric motors operated from indoors. The shutters for the second-story windows contain 1.75 in. of urethane. They may be slid laterally, manually. When not in use they are stored in slots within the walls. Use of the shutters reduces the overall night-time heat loss of the building by about 30%.

In summer the first-story south windows are shaded by a 4-ft overhang and the second-story south windows are shaded by the above-mentioned 2-ft-wide catwalk.

Heat exchanger. In winter much use is made of an air-to-air heat exchanger, 50-100 cfm with 80% efficiency, which not only exchanges stale air for fresh outdoor air but also prevents indoor humidity from becoming excessive.

Air change. Using a tracer gas technique, with 0°F outdoor temperature and with no actively induced air change, investigators found the change rate to be 5% per hour. Normally, forced air change is used, and any desired rate up to 80% per hour may be achieved. Recommended value in mid winter, with a typical family in residence, is 20% per hour.

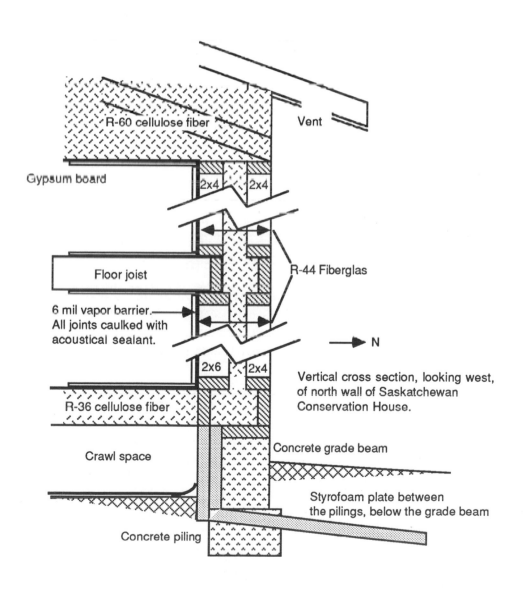

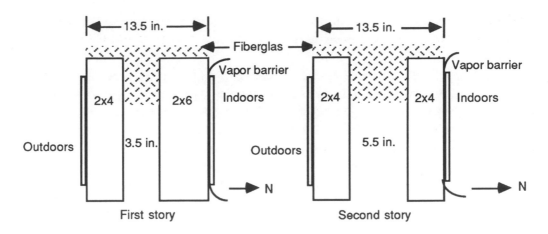

Vertical cross section, looking west, of south wall
of the Saskatchewan Conservation House

Active solar collector. The collector includes seven 8-ft x 4-ft panels of Owens-Illinois collector sloping 70 degrees from the horizontal. Gross area is 256 sq ft. Each panel includes 12 vacuum-jacketed tubes. The coolant, which is water, is drained at the end of each sunny day. (An earlier arrangement was to use a 67-33 mixture of water and ethylene glycol. Problems arose, and this arrangement was abandoned.)

Passive solar heating. An important amount of solar energy is received (as passive, direct-gain solar heating) via the first- and second-story south windows. The heat thus received is distributed throughout the house by means of a two-speed electric fan.

Auxiliary heat. There is no oil, gas or wood backup heating. When and if passive solar heating combined with intrinsic heat is not sufficient, heat may be taken (by a fan and coil) from the main thermal storage tank. Alternatively, one may merely turn on the top burners of the electric stove: they are adequate even for offsetting the peak heat loss of the building, which at -30°F is 3.7 kWh or 12,600 Btu/hr.

Storage system. 3,360 US gallons of water are stored in a 14-ft-tall cylindrical steel tank 6.5 ft in diameter, insulated to R-60, in the northwest corner of the house. If initially at 190°F, the tank contains enough heat to keep the house warm throughout a ten-day sunless mid-winter period. The tank includes an electrical heating element, but this has seldom been used. Indeed, the storage system itself has been put to little use other than heating the domestic hot water.

Domestic hot water. A 65-gal stone-lined tank with an internal heat exchanger and backup electrical heating elements is used. Heat is transferred to this tank from the main solar-heated storage tank by a centrifugal pump controlled by a thermostat.

PERFORMANCE AND RECOMMENDED CHANGES

The performance data have been corrupted by the fact that many thousands of visitors have inspected the building and opened doors numberless times. In other words, the conditions of use have been abnormal in the extreme.

Nevertheless, R.W. Besant and others of the Mechanical Engineering Department of the University of Saskatchewan have amassed much interesting information. The bottom line is that in a typical winter no heat is needed over and above what is supplied by intrinsic heat sources, passive solar heating, and active solar heating. More striking is the fact that the active solar heating system is scarcely needed: the annual amount of heat needed over and above intrinsic heating and passive solar heating (with no active solar heating) is about 3,700 kWh (about 12 MBtu).

The investigators found, in the winter of 1978-79 with the house unoccupied and virtually no intrinsic heating, that the heat-need was about 10,000 kWh or about 34 MBtu. Had there been a family in residence, the heat-need would have been only about one third as great.

On a typical night in winter, the actual gross rate of heat loss was 133 Btu/hr per 1°F of difference between indoor and outdoor temperature; that is, 70W/C.

The calculated value of effective thermal capacity of the house (not counting the large storage tank) is 10,800 Btu/°F; that is, 20.5 MJ/C.

The time rate of cooldown on a cold (-10°F) night with no intrinsic heating, with the shutters closed and the thermal storage tank not in use, was found to be 0.8 degrees per hour. This figure is consistent, give or take about 20%, with the measured value of heat-loss rate and the calculated value of effective thermal storage mass of the house proper.

In the light of trial use of this house and related studies, the following changes have been proposed for any future houses of this general type: Omit a big active solar heating system. Although designed primarily for space heating, it is not significantly needed for this purpose. Its main use is in heating domestic hot water, which could be accomplished by a much more modest solar-heating system. Use a different location for the vapor barriers serving the walls. Place them on the outer face of the inner set of studs, to avoid interference with the electrical wires.

Chapter 5

Components

All components of a superinsulated house must cooperate to produce comfort and health. These are paramount. Other goals are to keep heating and cooling bills low and minimize maintenance cost.

What is comfort? A dozen factors apply, but the main one is the temperature of room air. Most people like 65 to 70°F. Vigorous active people prefer 60°F, or even lower if they are moving about steadily. Older people prefer 70 to 75°F.

Such figures cannot be exact. Tastes differ. At different times of day a person prefers different temperatures. Also, his choice depends on several other factors, such as:

• The humidity of room air. When the humidity is very low, evaporation of moisture from the skin is rapid and has a cooling effect. Therefore a slightly higher air temperature is desired.

• The temperature of the walls. If the walls are very cold, they radiate less infrared radiation to the occupant's body than his body radiates to the walls. The net result is a cooling effect which must be offset by a higher room air temperature.

• The speed of air-flow past the occupant's body; that is, drafts. Airflow speeds exceeding one foot a second can produce noticeable cooling, again requiring a higher room air temperature.

• The amount of clothing worn, general rate of metabolism, degree of acclimatization.

Most people like the relative humidity of room air to be in the range 30 to 60%. Also, they like an inflow of fresh air—to dispel smells from kitchens, bathrooms, furnishings, cigarettes, human bodies, etc., and to eliminate any smoke that leaks from wood stoves. In some houses a more important need for fresh air is to get rid of gases that are harmful to health: for example, the radioactive gas radon.

Fortunately, all of these goals are easily achieved in a well designed superinsulated house that is equipped with an air-to-air heat-exchanger. Temperature and humidity are well controlled. There are no cold floors, no cold areas near windows, no drafts.

A bonus is that even if a total power failure occurs the superinsulated house will cool down only very slowly, will remain reasonably comfortable for a long time, and the danger of freezing and bursting pipes is almost entirely eliminated.

What about summer? The superinsulated house is especially easy to keep cool. The radiant temperatures of floors and walls on sunny days are lower than in conventional houses. The limited area of east and west windows and proper shading of south windows greatly reduce unwanted solar heating. In dry climates with relatively low night temperatures there may be no need for supplemental cooling. In more humid areas a ceiling fan may be needed to provide sufficient air movement. In the worst areas of high temperature and humidity, a combination of dehumidification and cooling may be required.

All these rewards are reaped only if the main components of the building have been designed and constructed properly. Today, after a decade of trial-and-error experience and countless intricate calculations made with modern computers, much is known as to ways of optimizing the designs of components.

WINDOWS

Great attention is given to reducing wintertime heat loss through windows. The main factors governing the use of windows in superinsulated houses are glazing, area, insulation, solar radiation control, air tightness, and safety.

Glazing

A typical single-glazed window of ordinary glass has an R-value of 0.9; thus the heat loss per square foot is about 30 to 50 times the loss per square foot of a well-insulated wall. Until the advent of high-performance glass, south windows needed to be double-glazed to provide R-1.8 (or triple-glazed to provide R-2.7, in very cold regions). East, west, and north windows needed to be double, triple, or quadruple glazed.

High performance windows are available. They combine special glasses with special films and gases between panes to reduce heat loss. It turns out that windows of ordinary type lose heat as much by far-infrared radiation as by simple conduction, and accordingly the manufacturers of new-type windows employ special coatings (or special films) that greatly reduce the energy-flow by far-infrared radiation; the special coatings reflect such radiation back into the room instead of allowing it to be transmitted to the outdoors. The special coated glass sheets, called low-e glass, are now made by several major glass producers. Special films also are in routine production; one of the best known is called Heat Mirror—a name that is not accurate because what is actually reflected is radiation, not heat.

Windows employing two sheets of glass in series, with an airspace between (preferably a space of at least a half inch), have an R value of about 2 (sq ft, hr/Btu) if no special coatings or films are used, and about 3 *with* coatings or films. Some architects prefer to use—instead of special coatings or films—three sheets of ordinary glass in series, or even four in very cold climates; thus they avoid questions as to cost or durability of the special coatings and films and questions as to availability of special shapes and sizes.

To reduce heat-loss by conduction, some manufacturers fill the (sealed) space between glass sheets with an inert gas (argon, for example) the molecules of which are so heavy and sluggish that they conduct heat very poorly. Such windows may have R-values as high as 8. However, questions of durability and cost remain. Time will tell whether such windows are good investments. (A key source of information is Interpane Coatings, Inc., PO Box 26, Deerfield WI 53531.)

Windows that have high R-values have the added merits of (a) greatly reducing the tendency of moisture to condense on the window glass and (b) making close-to-window room areas less chilly.

Providing Ample Daylight

In houses that have great width or many stories, there may be difficulty in arranging for enough daylight to reach the inner lower rooms. New techniques for improving the daylighting of such rooms have recently been developed. (They are described in recent issues of *DNNA News*, published by Daylighting Network of North America, c/o Prof. Fuller Moore, 125 Alumni Hall, Miami University, Oxford OH 45056. Cost of subscription: $20.00.) Some of the main strategies are: provide large windows, preferably extending high above floor level; paint the window sill and other faces white; use light-colored walls, floors, and carpets; install, within the window area, horizontal vanes (shelves) whose upper surfaces are mirror-like (or are painted white) and reflect much daylight to ceiling areas deep within the room; install skylights or clerestory windows. Some high-technology schemes proposed for especially wide and tall buildings employ special roof-top light-guiding mirrors, vertical light-conduits lined with reflecting surfaces, and horizontal light-distribution conduits serving inner lower rooms that otherwise would receive little or no daylight.

Area

The area of south windows should be moderate: large enough to admit much solar radiation on sunny days, but not so large that heat loss on cold nights is very large or heat gain on hot summer days is very large. Typically, with ordinary glazing, the south window area should be 5 to 10% of the floor area.

The window area on each other side of the house should be much less, only 1 or 2% of the floor area. Of course, if the main view happens to be to the west, say, a somewhat larger window area here is appropriate.

What can the designer do to make it feasible to use larger window areas? He can (1) use windows of especially high R-value, (2) provide thermal shades or shutters to be closed on cold nights, (3) provide wide eaves that will block the sun in summer. Also it may be desirable to increase the thermal masses of the sunlit floors or interior walls of the sunniest rooms.

Window Nighttime Insulation

In houses that are situated in cold climates and have windows that are only single- or double-glazed, the windows should be equipped with thermal shades (or shutters). These save heat, thus save money. Also they improve comfort.

Most such shades are operated manually. They are closed each evening and opened each morning. Automatic operation can be provided, but is complicated and expensive.

An ideal shade blocks the flow of heat by conduction, blocks the loss of energy by far-infrared radiation, and prevents warm-air leakage to the outdoors. This last capability is not needed if the windows themselve are airtight. Also, the shade should be attractive looking, durable, and easy to operate.

A great variety of shades are commercially available, each having its strong points and its weaknesses. Some very cheap types, employing clear plastic films taped to the window frame, perform fairly well but are not very durable or attractive. Some expensive types, employing a quilt that is unrolled in the evening and rolled up in the morning, provide fairly high R-value (about R-6 in combination with the double-glazed window) but are not fully sealed along all four edges. A device that is cheap and easy to make, install, and remove is a 1-in.-thick plate of Thermax (aluminum-foil-coated polyisocyanurate foam) that is simply cut with a knife to fit snugly within the window framing; it can be painted to match any room color scheme, and during the daytime can be stored entirely out of sight behind a bureau or bookcase; the plate adds about R-7 to the thermal resistance of the window system.

One interesting device that provides moderately high R-value, is inexpensive, is easy to install, and can be left on the window around the clock—day and night—is a three-layer, compartmentalized assembly of plastic sheets called Triplfilm. The films impart a slight amount of haziness to the view but are reasonably transparent. They are tightly sealed along all four edges, yet can be removed at any time, as for storage during the summer, and reinstalled later. (Supplier: Marshall Plastic Film Inc., Martin MI 49070.)

Should shades be on the inside (indoors) or outside (outdoors)? This issue has been debated for decades. Indoor shades may hurt the room appearance, and if they are not well edge-sealed, moisture may penetrate behind the shade, reach the cold window proper, and condense there, forming puddles and eventually damaging the sills. Outdoor shades are exposed to wind, rain, snow, freezing sleets and assorted wildlife (bees, squirrels, birds, and neighbors' children); and to operate such shades you must go outdoors—perhaps in the rain and in the dark—unless special through-the-wall controls are devised.

Thermal shades and shutters have been described in countless architectural, solar heating, and energy conservation magazines and in several books. (See Bibliography.)

Warning: All too many homeowners have installed expensive, high-performance, manually operated thermal shades—and then have been too lazy or forgetful to put them to use at night.

Use of Reflectors to Boost Solar Heating

The amount of solar radiation entering the house through its modest-size south windows can be greatly increased by providing, close outside the windowsill, a near-horizontal reflector (see sketch) consisting of, say, a sheet of plywood that has been covered with aluminum foil or has been painted white. Drawbacks are that the sheet may obstruct outdoor activities, and the sheet must be very securely anchored so as not to break loose in a windstorm. Of course, if the ground is covered by snow, the snow itself acts as a good reflector.

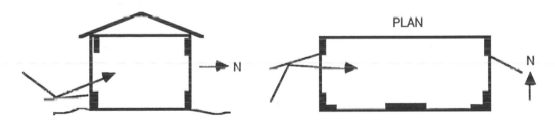

East and west windows may be equipped with vertical reflectors mounted at 45 degrees (see sketch); if they are hinged, they can be closed at night to reduce heat-loss.

Use of Eaves to Reduce Overheating in Summer

Summer overheating can be reduced by providing large overhang of the roof, which, ideally, would shade the south windows fully in summer and early fall but avoid shading them in winter and early spring. The most difficult period is early fall; the sun is then so low, even at noon, that the eaves may fail to shade the windows, and the outdoor temperature may far exceed 70°F. Ideally, one would have eaves that could be extended at such times, and retracted during the winter. Alternatively, adjustable awnings could be used.

Shading east and west windows is very difficult because the sun's rays reaching these windows are near horizontal. Eaves wide and low enough to block these rays would block the view also and would leave the rooms fairly dark. For such reasons, east and west windows are usually kept small—or omitted entirely.

WALLS

Recommended R-Values

The exterior walls of superinsulated houses are always heavily insulated—because the wall area is large (large potential heat loss) and installing thick insulation is easy.

Superinsulated houses in cold climates have wall R-values of at least 20, and usually 30 to 40. In Alaska, 40 to 60. The unit is $(ft^2$ hr F)/Btu.

A very detailed list of recommended R-values for houses in 100 different locations in the United States has been prepared by J.D. Balcomb (published in Passive *Solar Journal*, Vol. 3, No. 3, 1986, p. 221-248). He assumed that the houses had a reasonable amount of passive solar heating, and he listed recommended R-values for two different costs of auxiliary heating fuel: low and high. The R-values apply to the wall as a whole, not just the insulation proper. In using Balcomb's table, the designer picks a city near the proposed house site, makes a choice of fuel-cost category (high, for example), then finds from the table the conversion factor (CF) pertinent to these choices. He then multiplies this factor by the base number 14. The product is the recommended wall R-value. Example: For Boston, and assuming high fuel cost, one finds from the table that CF = 1.75. Thus the recommended R-value is (14)(1.75) = 24.5. For Minneapolis the recommended value is (14)(2.13) = 30.

This article includes corresponding information for ceilings, basements, and windows. The data are presented in tables and also maps of the United States.

Compromise Between R-Value and Cost

The optimum R-value depends on the cost of auxiliary heat (the higher the R-value, the more you save on auxiliary heat) and on the cost of insulation (the greater the amount of insulation used, the greater the cost of the insulation). A balance is needed. A rough rule is: if the cost of auxiliary heat increases10%, increase the R-value by 5%; and if the cost of insulation increases 10%, reduce the thickness by 5%. More exactly, the optimum R-value varies as the square root of the ratio of cost of auxiliary heat to cost of insulation. But the relationship can be thrown off by special circumstances involving the cost of extra studs, etc., cost of labor, interest rates, tax rates, and inflation.

Safety

The walls must conform to safety regulations. They must not contain materials that will give out noxious gases and they must not constitute a significant fire hazard. Fiberglass itself is non-flammable, and the same is true of aluminum-foil facing; but the kraft paper facing on some kinds of fiberglass rolls or batts can burn. Most foam-type insulating plates include fire inhibitors, but under severe conditions may burn; when they burn they emit poisonous gases. Cellulose fiber, unless it contains a sufficient quantity of fire inhibitor, can be a serious fire risk. (Warning:

Because superinsulated houses are tightly built, flammable gases can accumulate to high concentrations, creating the danger of a sudden and severe conflagration.)

Materials

Two widely used wall-insulating materials are fiberglass (rolls or batts) and cellulose fiber (wood fiber), which is blown into wall cavities. Both are inexpensive and easy to handle. Both have fairly low R-value per inch of thickness: about R-3. The exact value depends on the method of manufacture and the compactness of the installation. For example, compressing a thick fiberglass batt can increase the R-value *per inch* to about 4, although the thermal resistance of the batt as a whole is actually reduced (higher R-value per inch, but fewer inches!). A high-resistance wall employing fiberglass or cellulose fiber may be 6, 9, or even 12 in. thick—thick enough to reduce free floor area significantly (unless the exterior dimensions of the house are increased to avoid this).

Cellulose fiber is produced by so many companies that to list them would not be practical. The main manufacturers of fiberglass insulation are Owens-Corning Fiberglas Corp., Manville Corp., and Certain-Teed Corp. Various insulating materials having higher R-value per inch, and thus taking up less space for a given overall R-value, are often preferred, despite their greater cost.

Some of the best-known products are:

Isocyanurate foam board, usually aluminum-foil faced. R-7 to R-8 per in. Manufactured by: J. M. Walters Corp., Cellotex Div., called Thermax. Owens-Corning Fiberglas Corp., called High-R.

Expanded polystyrene foam board (EPS). Sometimes called beadboard. Many manufacturers. R-value about 4 per in. An aluminum-foil-faced type called Dura-R-Plus is made by Foam Plastics of New England, New Haven Rd., Prospect CT 06712.

Extruded polystyrene board. Several manufacturers, including Dow-Corning Corp., called Styrofoam. R-value about 5 per in.

Phenolic foam board, aluminum-foil faced. Manufactured by Koppers Co., Inc., called Rx insulating sheathing board. R-value about 8 per in. The material has superior fire resistance and higher cost.

Typical insulating plates of these materials are 1, 2, or 3 in. thick. Some kinds of plates have tongue-and-groove edges, to insure tight joints. Often tough adhesive tapes are used to make the joints airtight.

When these high-R-per-inch materials are used, the thickening of exterior walls is minimal. Typically, the walls are only 2 to 4 in. thicker than standard walls of 10 or 20 years ago.

Thin far-infrared-reflective foils are effective in some applications, especially when the goal is to prevent downward flow of heat from a hot roof or attic into the rooms below. Aluminum foil, if immediately adjacent to an airspace, is very effective in reducing energy flow by radiation (explained in *Energy Design Update* for May 1987, p. 12-15). The foil may increase the R-value of an insulating system by about 2 to 8.

Some of the main suppliers are:

Innovative Energy Inc., 1119 West 145 Ave., Crown Point IN 46307. Makes AstroFoil.

Energy Saver Imports, Inc., 2150 W. 6th Ave., Broomfield CO 80020. Distributes Foil-Ray.

Reflectix Inc., PO Box 108, Markleville IN 46056. Makes Reflectix.

Temperature Dependence of R-Value

The R-values of typical materials increase as the temperature of the materials decreases—because the molecules of air trapped within the materials move more slowly and conduct heat more poorly. If the temperature is decreased 10% (note: percent) on the absolute scale (scale using *absolute* zero as base), the resistance *increases* about 10%. To homeowners in very cold climates, this is a fine bonus!

Actual versus Nominal R-Value

The actual R-value of a wall may be much less than one would assume from the published R-values of the insulating materials used. Unintended and unsuspected cracks or gaps in the insulation—due to poor initial installation or subsequent shrinking—often occur, permitting heat to be lost in several ways: loss of heat by conduction, loss by within-wall convective air currents, and leakage of warm indoor air to the outdoors. The heat loss through a heavily insulated but carelessly constructed wall may be 20 to 35% greater than one would naively calculate. The presence of studs, headers, etc., also reduces the R-value of the wall as a whole.

Combination Systems

Some companies produce combination insulating-and-finishing assemblies, which combine high R-value with strength, toughness, weatherproofing, and good appearance. A great variety of such products is made by Dryvit System, Inc., One Energy Way, PO Box 1014, West Warwick RI 02893.

Structures That Accommodate the Extra Thickness

There are many different schemes for accommodating the extra insulation required for superinsulated houses. Each has its good and bad features. Heated debates have occurred at many conferences on building techniques, with no clear winners. The fact is that there are several successful strategies, and the choice depends strongly on availability and costs, in the given locality, of the special materials required, the experience of local construction workers, the local building codes, and the amount of money the prospective owner is willing to spend.

Several successful strategies are described below. In every case the designer must keep in mind:

• Strength of the wall.

• Avoidance of paths of easy heat-flow through the wall (that is, avoidance of thermal "short-circuits" or "thermal bridging"; there should be no wooden timbers extending all the way through the wall).

• Using, for the wall face toward the living space, a fireproof material—gypsum board (drywall) ordinarily.

• Preventing migration of moisture from the warm and humid room air into the cold outer region of the wall. A vapor barrier must be provided, and it must be situated much closer to the warm face of the wall than to the cold face so that it will always be warm enough so that no moisture will condense on it.

• Allowing space for electrical wires, plumbing pipes, etc., unless they can be located elsewhere.

Extra-wide studs. Instead of using 2x4 studs, the builder may use 2x6 or 2x8 studs. Thus the space avialable for insulation is about 6 or 8 in. thick instead of about 4 in. Because these studs are stronger than the usual studs, they can be placed farther apart: 24 in. on centers instead of 16. Thus the added cost of wider studs is partly offset by the use of fewer of them. This approach is simple, but has some drawbacks: The studs provide through-wall paths of easy heat flow, and there is no ready-made horizontal route for wires and pipes.

Studs with attached insulating plates. In this scheme, the builder first constructs an ordinary-appearing wall with 2x4 or 2x6 studs, drills holes through the studs to permit runs of wires and pipes, fills the between-stud spaces with fiberglass, and installs the vapor barrier. He then attaches to the toward-room face of the wall a one-inch or two-inch layer of insulating plate, such as Thermax, urethane or Styrofoam, and finally adds gypsum board. Result: high R, no through-wall paths or easy heat flow. Labor cost is low. Cost of added material is moderate.

Studs with horizontal straps and attached insulating plates. Here the builder first constructs an ordinary-appearing wall with 2x4s or 2x6s and fills the spaces with fiberglass; no holes are drilled. He then installs the vapor barrier. Next he attaches horizontal straps (2x2s, for example) to the toward-room face of the assembly, runs the wires and pipes close to the straps, fills the rest of the between-straps spaces with 2 in. of insulation (fiberglass or Styrofoam for example), and adds gypsum board.

Result: high R, no through-wall paths of easy heat flow, no need to drill holes through the studs, and the walls have added strength.

Double wall. Each complete wall (wall system) includes two individual walls: outer and inner. Each employs 2x4 studs that are 24 in. apart on centers. The studs of the inner wall are offset 12 in. with respect to those of the outer wall, so that no through-studs paths of easy heat flow exist. Typically the two walls are spaced so as to allow room (overall) for 9 in. of fiberglass or cellulose fiber insulation. The vapor barrier and gypsum board are attached, of course, to the toward-room face of the inner wall.

Although this method uses more wooden members and requires more labor, it is especially well suited to walls that must be extremely thick (9 to 14 in., say) in order to provide extremely high R-value. It was chosen for the Lo-Cal House, Leger House, and Saskatchewan Conservation House. It is used in advanced-construction houses in Scandinavia.

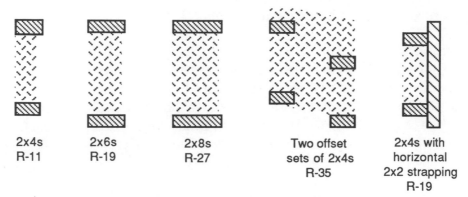

| 2x4s R-11 | 2x6s R-19 | 2x8s R-27 | Two offset sets of 2x4s R-35 | 2x4s with horizontal 2x2 strapping R-19 |

Horizontal cross sections of portions of exterior walls, with fiberglass insulation, showing several ways of achieving high R values.

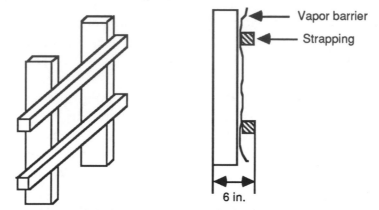

Portion of exterior wall employing 2x4 studs, vapor barrier, and horizontal 2x2 strapping (furring). The entire 6-in. space is to be filled with fiberglass. Not shown are Tyvek sheet, sheathing, and siding, at left, and gypsum board at right.

If double-wall construction is used, it is an easy matter to provide passageways for upward flow of any within-wall moisture into the within-eaves space; the moisture then flows through the attic vents to the outdoors.

Trusses. In some energy-efficient houses built in Canada and the United States, the builders provide an unusually thick wall space by using trusses, which may be 10, 12, 14 in. or more wide. A typical truss consists of two long stringers, about 2x2 in. in cross section, joined by a thin, light-weight web. The web may be a continuous strip of plywood, or several separate and spaced strips of plywood, or a set of diagonally-mounted metal connectors.

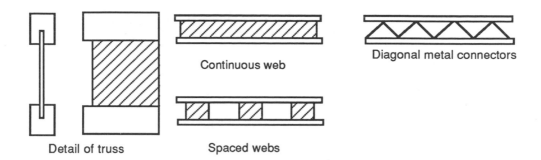

Detail of truss   Spaced webs   Continuous web   Diagonal metal connectors

The trusses made by Trus Joist Corporation have widths of 9.5 in. and 11-7/8 in.—to be used in place of ordinary lumber having nominal dimensions of 2x10 and 2x12. The stringers are made up of many thin laminations bonded permanently together, and the continuous plywood web is fitted tightly (and permanently bonded) into grooves in the stringers. The trusses are fabricated in lengths up to 60 ft. They are very true dimensionally and are light: A single man can easily lift a truss 40 ft long. There are many pre-cut easy-knock-out pieces in the web; these can be knocked out with a blow of a hammer to permit installing wires and pipes.

Some big producers of trusses and laminated wood beams are:

Trus Joist Corp. 9777 W. Chinden Blvd., PO Box 60, Boise ID 83707.

Wood Fabricators, Inc., Iron Horse Park, North Billerica MA 01862.

Prefabricated wall panels. Builders are increasingly making use of factory-made "stress skin" wall panels which, besides greatly speeding construction and providing excellent thermal performance, have considerable mechanical strength. A typical panel contains 3 or 4 in. of rigid foam sandwiched between rigid facing boards. The board that faces the room interior may be of gypsum or wood, and the board that faces the outdoors may be of plywood, chipboard, waferboard, particleboard, oriented-strand board, or other material.

The rigid foam may be of expanded polystyrene (EPS), which is especially inexpensive, or may be or urethane or isocyanurate foam, which have higher R-value and greater structural strength but are more expensive and harder to fabricate.

Panels that have waferboard faces have great structural strength, exceeding that of an ordinary 2x4 stud wall.

Adjacent panels may fit together in tongue-and-groove manner preferred by Foam Laminates of Vermont, or may be joined by splines or other mechanisms. Clamps may assist in anchoring panels together.

Before joining   After joining

Stress-skin panels with tongue-and-groove joints

Among the many manufacturers of prefabricated wall panels are:

Arcticor Building Systems Ltd., 21421 111 Ave., Winterburn, Alberta, Canada TOE 2N0.
Branch River Co., 15 Thurbers Blvd., Smithfield RI 02917.
Foam Laminates of Vermont, PO Box 102B, Hinesburg VT 05461.
Winter Panel Corp., RR 1, Box 161, Brattleboro VT 05301.

Sills, Headers, and Window Frames

The designer seeks to minimize heat-loss through the sills and headers of exterior walls and through the massive frames of windows. Usually an R-value of at least 5 is provided.

ATTIC AND ROOF

Typically, 10 to 12 in. of fiberglass or cellulose fiber is used in attics, giving R-35 to R-40. The insulation may rest on the attic floor or may be secured to the underside of the sloping roof. Why use more insulation in the attic than in the building walls? A dubious answer is: "Because heat tends to rise." A better answer is: "The attic surfaces are simple and clear: no windows, doorways, pipes; therefore installing thick insulation is very easy. Also, thick insulation here does not intrude on living space; it uses only space that is of little or no value." In very cold climates the fiberglass thickness may be increased to 16 in., to give R-50.

The height of the attic space at the eaves must be great enough so that (1) ample insulation may be installed here and (2) there is ample pathway for airflow—for example, flow of any moist air rising from within the exterior wall. Amply large vents are provided in the (under-eaves) soffits or along the roof ridge. Manufacturers provide a variety of such vents. A vapor barrier must be installed to prevent moist room air from penetrating into the cold upper regions of the attic insulation and causing condensation there.

In some houses, the roof is supported by a set of trusses, and trouble can arise if the lowest member of the truss is warm while the uppermost members are very cold: differential expansion may occur, causing the trusses to change shape (deform) and hurt the integrity of the room ceilings. Several strategies for avoiding this difficulty have been developed; they involve use of a dropped ceiling or uses of trusses that have dropped bases.

Note: Some builders have chosen not to allow outdoor air to flow into or from the attic in winter. They say that if vapor barriers insure that no moisture from the rooms can penetrate into the attic, no attic ventilation is needed; also if the attic is fully sealed, the attic air will be warmer and building heat-loss will be reduced.

Airflow Passages on Underside of Sloping Roof

If fiberglass batts are to be attached to the underside of a sloping roof, it is usually desirable to provide, between roof and batts, a passage, or channel, for airflow. Then air that enters via soffit vents can flow upward, in such channels, to the ridge vent. To insure that clear channels exist between roof and batts, many builders install slim troughs on the underside of the roof. These keep the batts an inch or two from the roof proper.

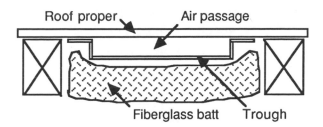

Roof proper   Air passage

Fiberglass batt   Trough

An example of such a trough is Dura-Foam Rafter-Vent produced by Foam Plastics of New England, New Haven Rd., Prospect CT 06712. The troughs, of expanded polystyrene, are stapled to the underside of the roof—before the batts are installed.

FLOOR OF FIRST STORY

If the house has an insulated basement, no insulation is required in the floor of the first story. If the basement is not insulated, insulation should be installed on the underside of this floor. Fiberglass or insulating board (such as urethane) may be used—enough to provide, say, R-19 to R-30.

FOUNDATION WALL, BASEMENT, CRAWL SPACE

Designers now realize that it is important to provide good insulation for foundation or basement walls, unless the first-story floor itself is to be insulated. Usually the insulation, consisting of 2 in. of Styrofoam for example, is applied to the exterior of the wall; thus the wall itself remains warm and contributes importantly to the thermal mass of the house; also, the insulation is well protected. Alternatively the insulation can be installed on the within-building face of the wall; but it may then need to be sheathed for mechanical protection, and it leaves the concrete walls cold with the consequences that they do not contribute to thermal mass and if any moist air penetrates through the insulation and reaches them condensation will occur. For these reasons most designers choose the exterior location.

In installing insulation on the exterior, provision must be made for allowing ground water reaching the insulation to drain readily downward to the drainage pipes at the base of the wall. Downward flow is facilitated by any of the following:

• Loose stone fill: coarse gravel or crushed rock.

• Special fiberglass batts, the fibers of which are oriented parallel to wall and thus permit easy downward flow (and negligible flow toward the wall). Such batts, called Warm-N-Dri, are produced by Owens Corning Fiberglas Corp., Fiberglas Tower, Toledo OH 43659. Between batt and wall, an asphaltic membrane called Tuff-N-Dri is installed.

• Special boards of bonded insulating granules that, besides providing R-3.5 thermal insulation per inch, permit downward flow of water. Such boards are produced by Geotech Systems Corp., 100 Powers Court, Sterling VA 22170, and are called Geotech Insulated Drainage Board.

• A nylon fiber matt, called Enkadrain, made by BASF Corporation Fibers Division, Geomatrix Systems, Enka NC 28728.

In backfilling the excavation after the insulation has been applied, the contractor must be careful not to break or crush the insulation.

In some instances, the basement floor itself is insulated. Or insulation may be applied just to the outer 3 ft. of this floor, that is, just close to the exterior walls.

An exterior-insulated basement wall of concrete requires no vapor barrier, although the first-story floor should have a vapor barrier if the basement is to be allowed to remain fairly cold for long periods.

The earth floor of a crawl space should be covered with a vapor barrier unless the first-story floor is to include a vapor barrier. Often, if the earth floor is covered with a vapor barrier, there is no need to vent the crawlspace.

Some companies supply equipment that greatly simplifies the construction of an insulated wall of poured concrete. The equipment consists of forms (to contain the liquid concrete) that themselves consist of expanded polystyrene foam. One sets the inner and outer forms in place, installs connector wires to prevent them from spreading, then pours the concrete. Result: a sturdy and fully insulated wall.

One manufacturer of the special forms is RVG Thermal Wall Co., PO Box 261, Chatham NY 12037. A company called Form Products Inc., of Naperville, IL, produces forms that consist of 2-inch-thick polystyrene blocks that are castellated and tongue-and-groove-equipped for quick assembly.

EXTERNAL DOORS AND AIR-LOCK ENTRIES

External doors should, obviously, be of high-R type. Typical doors of decades ago had R-values of only about 1 or 2. Today, R-6 to R-12 is a good goal. Manufacturers now supply a variety of attractive high-R doors. They should be tightly fitted and/or weatherstripped. Doors of especially high R-value (R-15) are made by The Stanley Works, 195 Lake St., New Britain CT 06050.

The requirements on exterior doors may be eased somewhat if air-lock entries, or vestibules, are provided. Such vestibules, beside greatly reducing heat loss via the doors, may be large enough to include coat-and-boot closets or may serve as utility rooms. In some cases the air-lock function may be served by an attached sunspace, greenhouse, or garage.

Many—most?—architects have concluded that air-lock entries are not worthwhile. In mid-winter, occupants enter or leave only a few times a day, and the brief bursts of fresh, low-humidity air may be welcome. Also, occupants may be careless and leave the inner door of the airlock open at times, thus defeating the purpose of the air-lock.

Chapter 6
Barriers to Infiltration

AIR/VAPOR BARRIERS

One of the most important and most-discussed components of a superinsulated house is the vapor barrier, or air/vapor barrier. Such barriers perform two important functions:

1. They prevent room-air moisture from reaching the cold parts of exterior walls, ceilings, etc. (cold parts of the insulation, cold framing members, etc.) and condensing there, forming pools of water or ice, degrading the performance of the insulation and perhaps eventually leading to rotting of wooden studs, sills, etc.

2. They prevent air leaks to or from the room and thus avoid unnecessary heat loss.

It is now generally believed that the main mechanisms of travel of moisture to cold regions of walls, etc., are slender airflow streams. Travel purely by diffusion (by individual molecular motion without any net airflow) is extremely slow and so plays only a secondary role. In summary, the primary function of the vapor barrier is to prevent flow of room air into the cold walls. The secondary function is to prevent moisture diffusion.

How effective must the vapor barrier be in stopping diffusion of moisture? The usual criterion is that the water-vapor permeance must be less than 1.0. This goal is met easily by polyethylene ("poly") sheets or films and by aluminum foil; these have a perm rating below 0.1. [Note: the perm is defined as 1 grain of gaseous H_2O per (sq ft, 24-hr-day, inch Hg pressure)].

Usual Materials

Usually the vapor barrier consists of a polyethylene sheet 0.006 inches (6 mils) thick. The large and long rolls of such sheets should be stored—before installation—indoors; exposure to the blue and ultraviolet components of daylight may initiate chemical changes that, after some years, may cause embrittlement and tearing, with the result that the barrier will fail to perform its functions. UV-stabilized brands of polyethylene are available, as are extra-tough brands that employ chemical cross-linking. Some brands are opaque (black), and are especially resistant to UV radiation; other brands are transparent, which makes it easy for building inspectors to examine the wall construction and insulation even after the vapor barrier has been installed.

So many companies make polyethylene sheet that to list their names and addresses is impractical. A type that is weather resistant and pin-hole free, called Tu-Tuf Cross-Laminated Poly Sheeting, is produced by Sto-Cote Products, Inc., PO Drawer 310, Richmond IL 60071. A high-quality type, called Tenoarm, that meets strict Swedish standards is available from Resource Conservation Technology, Inc., 2033 N. Calvert St., Baltimore MD 21218; it is extra thick (0.008 in.), and has especially low permeance and outstanding durability.

Some foam-type insulating boards are aluminum-foil faced. This is true of Thermax, for example. Such boards can serve as vapor barriers if all of the edges of the boards are sealed with aluminum tape or the equivalent.

Can paint serve as a vapor barrier? Yes: for example, a paint called Insul-Aid and sold by Glidden Durkee Division of SCM Corp. is very effective. It may be procured from the main company, at 3rd and Bern Sts., Reading PA 19603, or, in New England, from a branch at 155 Main St., Stoneham MA 02180. Some oil-base paints and some other types are effective; for example: Moore's Alkyd Primer Sealer, Sear's Best Oil Base Primer 5881, and B-I-N Primer Sealer.

These paints are especially effective if two coats are used. To be avoided are most common types of paint—latex paints, especially.

Location of Application

In cold climates, vapor barriers are usually placed on the *warm* sides of walls, ceilings, etc. However, an alternative location is permissible and, in some instances, preferable: a location such that one third of the insulation is on the warm side of the barrier and two thirds is on the cold side. So situated, the barrier will nearly always be warm enough so that no moisture will condense on it; and the builder is now free to install pipes, wires, outlet boxes, etc., within the shallow region on the warm side of the barrier.

In very hot climates the vapor barrier may be placed on the *outer* side of the wall, to help exclude moisture threatening to enter from outside on very hot and humid days when the rooms themselves are kept cool.

Seals

Sealing the vapor barriers along their edges is important. Normally the builder overlaps adjacent barriers (sheets) 3 to 6 inches and staples and seals the overlap. The overlap should occur where there is a solid backing, that is, immediately in front of a stud or header or equivalent. The usual sealant used is "acoustical seal" which remains elastic indefinitely. (It is made by Tremco, 10701 Shaker Blvd., Cleveland OH 44104. This company is said to have, also, other kinds of adhesives that are gun-applied, perform excellently, and are "cleaner" to use.) Other companies make fully satisfactory adhesives; butyl rubber sealants, for example, perform well and have a very long useful life, despite their tendency to harden.

Instead of using a gun-applied sealant, one may use sealing tape, such as 3M Company's No.8086 Contractor Sheathing Tape, easily applied to polyethylene or Tyvek using the 3M H-75 Hand Dispenser (supplied by 3M Contractor Products, 3M Center, St. Paul MN 55144-1000).

Backing

Some builders are convinced that it is important that the vapor barrier have, throughout at least most of its area, a firm backing—a backing that is sufficiently rigid to prevent the vapor barrier sheet from moving, bellying, etc., when there is a very high wind that produces some "mini-gusts" within the wall. If the vapor barrier bellies repeatedly, gaps may soon arise at the edges, and possibly the sheet will rip or tear.

Maintenance of Integrity

Vapor barriers are of first importance. Builders of superinsulated houses must recognize the need for giving much attention, and close supervision, to the barrier and making sure that its moisture-proof integrity is complete. In typical houses of some years ago, vapor barriers were relatively unimportant; abundant leakage of air would, before long, carry away any condensed moisture. But to the success of a superinsulated house, vapor barriers are essential.

It is imperative that holes and gaps be sealed. Gaps are especially likely to occur where water pipes, wires, chimneys, vent pipes, etc., pass through the barrier. These gaps must be found and sealed. The problem is simplified if the pipes, wires, etc., can be routed so as not to encounter the barriers. For example, the builder may arrange for there to be no electrical wires within any exterior wall; outlet boxes may be limited to partition walls, or provided by wiring strips on the toward-room faces of exterior walls, that is, strips everywhere within the space defined by the barriers.

If the builder decides to use no polyethylene sheet but to use aluminum-foil-faced Thermax as a vapor barrier, he must keep in mind the possibility that the Thermax plates may shrink or warp or for some other reason deform, leaving cracks between plates. Some builders consider it safer to use polyethylene sheets.

Obviously, the requirement on integrity of vapor barrier can be greatly relaxed if the house is in a mild climate and the indoor humidity remains low. Even in cold climates some relaxation is permissible if the house ventilation system is such that indoor air pressure is slightly below outdoor air pressure; such pressure differential tends to produce a slight inflow of (cold dry) outdoor air through any cracks in the exterior walls, and this inflow will tend to dry out the within-wall regions.

Curiously enough, relatively few instances of harmful moisture deposition within walls have been reported by builders.

Electrical Boxes

When electrical boxes are attached to an exterior wall, they must be joined to the vapor barrier. Otherwise, much moist air can pass into the cold within-wall region. Most builders enclose the box within a plastic "hat" that is sealed to the vapor barrier. Alternatively the builder can employ an air-vapor-barrier electrical box (such as that produced by R & S Vapour Seal Systems, RR #2, Boyers Rd., Keswick, Ontario Canada L4P 3E9).

Airtight Drywall Approach

In the early 1980s two Canadian engineers, J.W. Lstiburek and J.K. Lischkoff, developed a new way of preventing room-air moisture from penetrating into exterior walls. Their method, called the Airtight Drywall Approach, or ADA, is to rely on tightly joined and specially coated gypsum boards (drywall), the boards regularly used on wall interior faces and on ceilings. If all of the board-to-board joints are tightly made and if a moisture-impermeable coating is applied to all of the boards, no moisture can reach the cold within-wall regions; no polyethylene film is needed. (For details, see Ref. L-400 and also *Popular Science* for Dec. 1986, p. 81-82.)

The proponents claim, for the new method, two big advantages: (1) There is no plastic film that may deteriorate within 5, 10, or 20 years—as for example if the film becomes brittle and cracks as a result of pre-installation exposure to sunlight or other not-fully-understood factors. The home owner may not know that the film has deteriorated, and if it does deteriorate there is no easy way to get at it to replace it. (2) The crucial surfaces (of the gypsum boards) are fully visible, are easily inspected, and can easily be repaired.

Many houses have been built with the ADA method. In general they have been found to perform well. But because special construction methods and special care are required, some groups that have made trial use of the system have found that overall cost may be increased. Thus the long-term prospects for ADA are uncertain.

EXTERNAL AIR-AND-WATER BARRIERS

In the last few years many builders have adopted the practice of including, in the *outer* portions of exterior walls, a barrier that, while *permeable* to airborne moisture (gaseous water), is *impermeable* to air currents and liquid water. The function of this barrier is to prevent strong winds from driving cold outdoor air into the within-wall regions via cracks, etc., and to prevent rainwater from entering those regions. If outdoor air enters the wall insulation, even without penetrating through the wall and into the room, it can greatly reduce the effective R-value of the wall insualtion.

If such a barrier were impermeable to gaseous water, any within-wall moisture would be permanently trapped there—by this barrier on the outside and the vapor barrier near the inside. But the external air-and-water barrier usually used—duPont's Tyvek™—is, fortunately, somewhat permeable to gaseous water; it has a rating of 90 perms. It is permeable because it is not a continuous film but consists of a mat of fibers ("spun olefin").

A competing product, also of spun olefin, is called Barricade. (It is made by Simplex Products Division, PO Box 10, Adrian MI 49221-0010. This material, and other kinds, is listed and compared in *Energy Design Update* for April 1987, pp. 5-8.)

NATURAL INFILTRATION

In every house there is some natural inflow of fresh air. No house is hermetic. Fresh air may enter via cracks in foundations, walls, window frames, roof, etc. Also it may enter via cracks at tops, bottoms, and sides of outside doors. It may enter via chimneys associated with a furnace, cooking stove, or wood stove. It may enter via vents associated with kitchen or bathroom air-exhaust systems, or via vents intended mainly for use in summer. Occupants may leave windows open. Children may leave outside doors open.

The subject has been investigated by many engineers here and abroad, and there are many interesting reports on the subject. (Some are available through Air Infiltration and Ventilation Center, Old Bracknell Lane, Bracknell, Berkshire, Great Britain RG 12 4 AH. An excellent report by A. K. Blomsterberg and D. T. Harrje, "Approaches to Evaluation of Air Infiltration Energy Losses in Buildings," has been published in *ASHRAE Transactions, 85*, 1979, Part 1.)

Causes

Natural infiltration is a consequence of wind and chimney effect (stack effect). These provide the driving forces. Wind, or the pressure produced by it, drives air into a house on the upwind side of it. The air enters via cracks, holes, etc. Of course, nearby buildings, trees, shrubs, etc., tend to slow the wind; "wind reduction factors" of 0.7 to 0.9 are common. (See Ref. L-200.) Chimney effect (tendency of warm air to rise) causes warm air to escape from the upper part of a house and cold outdoor to enter the lower part.

On a windy day, the natural infiltration in a one-or-two story house is largely due to wind effect. But on a calm day in midwinter the natural infiltration in a multi-story house is largely due to chimney effect. When there is no wind and the outdoor and indoor temperatures are equal, there is no natural infiltration.

Of course, the inflow of cold outdoor is increased when a kitchen or bathroom exhaust fan is turned on, or when a typical furnace or woodstove is operated and discharges much stack air to the outdoors. (Today, some furnaces and stoves have special supplies of air—ducted air—and thus do not tend to increase the inflow of outdoor air via cracks, etc.)

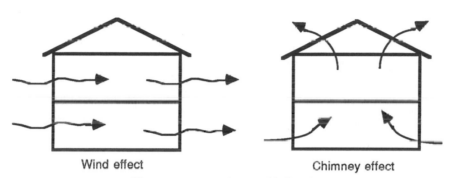

Wind effect   Chimney effect
The two causes of natural infiltration

Flowrates

The amount of infiltration may vary enormously from day to day and even hour to hour, depending on speed and direction of wind, extent to which windows and vents are left open, and extent to which exhaust fans, furnaces, etc. are in use. Cracks may be wider during very dry periods and narrower during moist periods inasmuch as wood tends to give off or take up H_2O during very dry or very humid periods—and has a slightly greater volume when it contains much H_2O.

Of course, the amount of *exfiltration* equals the amount of *infiltration*. Otherwise the house would threaten to explode or implode! Usually it suffices to talk just about the *infiltration*.

How does the rate of airflow through a crack or small hole vary with the pressure head ΔP? The answer depends on the type of flow: Is it turbulent or laminar (smooth)? It is turbulent if the speed of the air in the crack is high and the crack width is great—and it is laminar if the speed is low and the crack is slender. The following formulas—in metric units—apply:

Turbulent flow: $Q = k (\Delta P)^{0.5}$
Laminar flow: $Q = k (\Delta P)^{1.0}$

where Q is the flow in cubic meters per second, ΔP is the pressure head, or pressure difference in Pascals, and k is a constant that depends on the dimensions of the crack.

In a typical house there are many cracks, these have a big range of widths, and the pertinent formula is a compromise that has an exponent that is about 0.65:

$$Q = k (\Delta P)^{0.65}$$

These formulas hold very closely when moderate to large pressure heads are involved— 3 to 50 Pascals—but are only roughly correct for small pressure heads such as 0 to 2 Pascals, typical of pressures experienced on calm mild days. For that range, other formulas have been developed. (See Liddament, L-200 in the Bibliography.)

Tracer-Gas Method of Measurement

The tracer-gas method of measuring the infiltration rate starts with the sudden release, into the air in the house, of a small quantity of a special gas: a gas that is (a) different from all other gases present in room air, (b) easily detected even at very low concentrations, (c) stable, and (d) non-toxic. After releasing the tracer gas, the investigator uses one or more fans to distribute the gas uniformly throughout the house, i.e., to mix it thoroughly with all of the indoor air.

He then measures the concentration of the tracer gas at the end of each 15-minute or 30-minute time interval. Each measurement is made on an air sample that is a composite of small amounts collected in different rooms and thus is representative of the indoor air as a whole. Successive measurements show, of course, successively lower concentrations of the tracer gas.

The investigator then plots a graph of tracer-gas concentration as a function of time. From the graph the investigator can at once determine the rate at which fresh air was entering the house, in house volumes per hour. This result, if no exhaust fans or air-to-air heat-exchanger was in operation, is the natural infiltration rate under the given conditions of wind and outdoor temperature.

One commonly used tracer gas is sulfur hexafluoride, SF_6, which, when dispersed in room air, can be detected even when present in very small amounts, such as a few parts per billion. Under normal conditions of use as tracer, this gas is stable, odorless, and non-toxic. Ordinarily there is none of it in room air. An extremely sensitive detection method is used: a method involving capture, by the SF_6 molecules, of electrons that have a certain energy. The equipment is called a gas chromatograph. A carrier gas—argon—facilitates the measurement process.

Before the test is begun, a preliminary test is made to see whether any freon is present in the room air. If any freon is present, it can greatly interfere with the detection of SF_6 inasmuch as these two materials have somewhat similar electron capture capabilities.

The main measurement is started by releasing about 10 cubic centimeters of SF_6 gas into the room air—say a ground-floor room on the upwind side of the house. Fans are then used to distribute the tracer gas uniformly throughout the indoor air. The SF_6 concentration is then measured every 15 or 30 minutes, and, from a graph of the results, the investigator computes the infiltration rate.

Various other gases, including methane, nitrous oxide, and radioactive krypton have been used. (See Report LBL-8394 published by the Lawrence Berkeley Laboratory of the University of California, "An Intercomparison of Tracer Gases Used for Air Infiltration Measurements," by D.T. Grimsrud and others.)

Measurement of Equivalent Leakage-Hole Area; Blower-Door Tests

In recent years, the practice of using "blower doors" to measure the leakiness of a house has become very common. The method is simple, quick, and highly revealing. An investigator installs a large variable-speed fan in an outer door of the house (a special door that temporarily replaces the normal door) and runs the fan at such a speed as to produce a moderately high overpressure of indoor air—which in turn produces a high rate of leakage of room air to the outdoors via cracks, holes, etc.

If the house is very leaky, the fan must run at high speed to produce the chosen degree of overpressure; if the house is tight, the fan may run at low speed and still produce it. By finding the appropriate fan speed, and consulting a calibration chart, the investigator can estimate the aggregate area of the crack, holes, etc. Usually he expresses the result in terms of the diameter of a single hole that would result in leakage such as has been measured. For example, he may conclude that a single hole 10 inches in diameter would provide the observed leakage.

Often the investigator prefers to reverse the fan and create, in the house, a pressure that is *below* atmospheric pressure. Or he may first use overpressure, then underpressure, and compare the results.

Immediately on finding that the leakage rate in a given house is higher than it should be, the investigator may set to work to find the main leakage paths (he may use small titanium-tetrachloride smoke generators to make the tiny airflows visible) and to close off these paths by means of caulking materials, tapes, or other means. Then he can repeat the pressurization test and find what improvement has been made.

How great an overpressure (or underpressure) is used? A frequent choice is 50 pascals, corresponding to about 0.2 in. of water. Of course, such a pressure produces air leakage far greater than occurs naturally under typical conditions; a very rough rule of thumb is that the leakage at 50 pascals corresponds to the leakage that occurs naturally when the house in question is subjected to 25-to-30 mph winds.

Many builders of superinsulated houses make blower-door tests routinely after a new house has been nearly completed—completed enough so that its tightness should meet the builder's goal. Anticipating such tests, the construction crews work especially hard to give the house a high score. If the test result is low, they must recheck their work and improve the tightness.

Does the blower-door test provide a value of natural infiltration rate? Yes and no. If the test shows that there is only an extremely small equivalent leakage area, then it is certain that the natural infiltration rate is low. But if the test shows that the leakage area is great, the infiltration rate may remain in doubt. This is because the blower-door test fails to show the crack or hole locations. If there were one large hole on an upwind side of the house and another large hole on the downwind side, this could cause much infiltration. But if there were several large holes on the same side of the house (or if all of the holes were in the basement), the amount of infiltration might be less by a factor of 5 or 10. Thus, although much effort has been given by various research groups to finding a correlation between blower-door test results and tracer-gas-test results, it is unlikely that any close correlation will ever be found.

If a designer insists on using a correlation number, the number 20 may be about as good as can be found (according to a 1986 article by Alan Meier, in *Energy Auditor and Retrofitter*, July-Aug. 1986). Thus if blower-door tests made at a pressure of 50 pascals show an air change rate of 20 house volumes per hour, one may guess that the natural infiltration rate is about 20/20 or 1 ACH.

Despite the difficulty in making overall interpretations, blower-door tests are likely to be used increasingly—because (1) such tests boost the morale of the building crews, (2) they motivate and assist the search for leaks and efforts to close off the leaks, and (3) if the blower-door test shows a very low leakage rate, a very low infiltration rate is assured.

Some major manufacturers of blower-door equipment are:

Minneapolis Blower Door, 920 W. 53 St., Minneapolis MN 55419. Tel: (612) 827-1117; also (612) 929-6949. Sells blower door that provides airflow rates from 40 to 6000 cfm, fits easily into a small car, weighs 50 lbs., and costs about $1250.

Retrotec USA, 6215 Morenci Trail, Indianapolis IN 46268. Tel: (800) 422-0923; also (317) 297-1927. Sells blower doors, priced from about $1,000 to $6,000, smoke pencils, priced at about $3, and smoke guns, priced at about $70.

Ener-Corp Management Ltd., 2 Donald St., Winnipeg, Manitoba, Canada R3L 0K5. Its distribution network is called "Ener-Seal."

Canadian Book on Sealing Techniques

A very detailed book on the principles and methods of sealing houses so as to make them almost perfectly airtight has been prepared under the auspices of the Building Energy Technology Transfer Program (BETT Program) of the Canadian Dept. of Energy, Mines and Resources. Prepared by Marbek Resource Consultants of Ottawa, this 300-pp book describes, in words and drawings, almost every possible way of sealing all major components of energy-efficient houses. (See Bibliography, E-450.

Chapter 7

Thermal Mass
and Auxiliary Heat

THERMAL MASS

Two factors govern the rate at which a house cools down during a cold (0°F, say) period in winter when no heat is supplied to the house: the thermal mass of the house and the thermal resistance of external walls, windows, roof, etc. If the product of these two quantities is large, the house will cool down only very slowly. An added benefit of large thermal mass is that if, with the house already reasonably warm, much solar radiation enters, the house warms up only a few degrees and the occupants will not feel compelled to open windows to cool off; they are content to have the energy remain in the house, and the energy will be useful in keeping the house warm during the coming cold night.

In many direct-gain solar houses of ten years ago the thermal resistance was small and accordingly the designers were obliged to provide much added thermal mass: stone-faced floor, concrete or brick partition walls, arrays of water-filled containers, etc. But in a superinsulated house the insulation is superb, thermal resistance is high, and so it is permissible for the thermal mass to be small—of the order of 15,000 to 30,000 lb such is supplied by the typical amounts of wood, gypsum board, concrete basement, etc. What actually counts, of course, is the *effective* thermal mass: the mass of components that heat up and cool down as the room air itself heats up and cools down. Components outside the insulating envelope do not contribute to effective thermal mass.

Example: Saskatchewan Conservation House

Here the wall components, floor components, ceiling components, etc., that are thermally isolated from outdoors and thermally coupled to room air have a mass of 22,000 lb and a heat-storage capacity of about 10,800 Btu/F. A list of the contributions is given in the chart on the next page.

Excluded from the list are all components *outside* the insulation. Thus the outer set of studs and all material farther out than these are excluded. Likewise the floor joists of the first story are excluded. All components of the large (unheated) attic and (unheated) crawlspace are excluded. Also the large steel storage tank is excluded.

Note that about two thirds of the effective thermal capacity is attributable to wood and about one fourth is attributable to gypsum board.

Component	Mass		Thermal capacity		
	kg	lb	MJ/°C	Btu/°F	Percent
Gypsum board	5,006	11,000	5.5	2,900	27%
Wood studs	2,072	4,600	3.9	2,050	
flooring	2,034	4,500	3.9	2,050	63%
floor joists	2,286	5,000	4.3	2,260	
ceiling joists	453	1,000	0.9	470	
Furniture and appliances	1,000	2,200	2.0	1,054	10%
TOTALS	12,951	28,300	20.5	10,800	100%

How to Increase the Mass

If a designer is insistent on increasing the thermal mass of a superinsulated house he is designing, he could, for example, use two layers of gypsum board, rather than just one. The second layer, behind the layer that is visible in the room, may be of gypsum boards that are partly broken (rejects) and in a sense are free (suggested by R. W. Besant). Also, the builder could make some of the partition walls of bricks or concrete blocks. Of course, water-filled containers could be used. Preferably the added mass is placed where it will receive direct sunlight or placed closely adjacent to such locations.

AUXILIARY HEAT

Some superinsulated houses, even in the colder regions of the contiguous United States, may get through the winter without need for auxiliary heat. Heat from intrinsic sources and direct-gain passive solar heating may provide 100% of the heat needed. More often, of the order of 10 million Btu may be required of an auxiliary system. This is about as much as would be provided by burning about 100 gal of oil (roughly $100 worth) in a 67%-efficient furnace.

If, in a superinsulated house, the auxiliary heat is discharged at some central location, it may diffuse throughout the house fast enough so that no special distribution system is needed. If hallways are short, doorways are wide and are usually left open, diffusion may be fully adequate. Distribution can be facilitated by providing additional openings between rooms and halls. If the bottom inch of every door is cut off, the resulting gaps will allow some circulation of air even when the doors are closed. Of course, circulation can be speeded by use of one or two small fans; even 4-inch-diameter 15-watt fans can help considerably.

What is the best way of supplying a small amount of auxiliary heat? There are many options. None is perfect. Several are fully adequate.

Furnaces and wood stoves. Many kinds of small gas furnaces are available, are low in cost, and are high in efficiency. Troubles sometimes arise (surveyed in *Energy Design Update* for April 1987). Or buy a small oil-type furnace, an oil tank, and a heat distribution system. Build a chimney. Plenty of heat can then be provided. But there are many troubles. The system may cost $3,000 to $5,000. The system is likely to be far oversized; very small oil furnaces are non-existent, or nearly so. Operating and maintaining a furnace can be a nuisance. Furnaces can misbehave: produce smoke that might spread throughout the basement, or possibly present a fire hazard. If the electrical power should fail, as in some widespread emergency, the furnace would not run.

Buy and install a wood-burning stove. This may work well if the stove is of properly designed type, is nicely installed, and is capable of being closed off so as to cause no leakage of air when not in use. Preferably it should be supplied with ducted air. But a poorly designed stove, improperly installed, can cause troubles of many kinds.

Kerosene and electric heaters. Small heaters in which kerosene is burned are inexpensive and produce the desired small amount of heat. They need no chimney, merely a wall vent. Recent models burn cleanly and include important safety features. But many experts continue to worry that incorrect use or faulty maintenance could lead to fire hazards, and the combustion products might under some circumstance create a health hazard, especially in a well-sealed superinsulated house.

Buy one or two portable electric heaters equipped with thermostats and install them at two central locations in the house. Cost of equipment is low, the amount of space required is small, operation is automatic, and no fumes or smells are produced. The danger of fire is minimal unless the house occupants allow clothing, papers, etc. to come in close contact with the heaters. Excellent results are obtained with electrical heaters that consist of white panels mounted close beneath the ceiling, well out of the way of furniture, etc. They warm the entire room by means of infrared radiation.

Such panels are produced, for example, by Solid State Heating Corp., 49 Day St., South Norwalk CT 06856. The main drawback to electrical heaters is that electrical power is costly; but if the amount of heat needed is small the cost is not important. The cost will be especially small if the local utility charges lower rates for nighttime (off-peak) electricity use and if the heaters are used mainly at off-peak times.

A better performance is obtained if one employs electric baseboard heaters. Better heat distribution results, and fire hazards are further reduced. The equipment cost, however, is greater.

Domestic hot water systems and heat pumps. In the Leger House in East Pepperill MA, double use was made of the gas-type domestic-hot-water heater: a Paloma wall-mounted device about the size and shape of a full knapsack. The heater heats the water in a well-insulated 40-gallon domestic hot water tank, which (1) supplies hot water to kitchen and bathroom, and (2) supplies hot water to a 40-ft-long baseboard radiator whenever room temperature falls below 70°F. The system performs the two functions without difficulty. (Warning: one must make sure that the circulation of hot water to the baseboard radiators cannot pollute the water in the tank; as a last resort one can install in the tank a small water-to-water heat-exchanger of special type that can never allow the circulated water to mix with the tank water.)

A similar scheme may be applied to an electric-type domestic hot water system. One tank of hot water can serve kitchen, bathrooms, and baseboard radiators. Operating cost can be reduced if most of the heating of the tank is done at off-peak hours and off-peak (low) rates are available.

Instead of a baseboard radiator a small fan-and-coil system could used. A "Chill Chaser" system, for example.

One could deliver heat from the tank by a small stream of air: a small blower could circulate air around the body of the tank—just *inside* the insulating jacket—then deliver this air to the rooms by a 4-inch-diameter flexible duct. It would be necessary to enlarge the jacket so as to leave a one- or two-inch space between tank wall and jacket. Such a scheme would eliminate any possibility of polluting the tank water.

Space heating could be provided by means of an especially small heat pump that would extract heat from the ground, or from ground water, and deliver the heat to the rooms.

Tomorrow's improved systems. Several kinds of auxiliary heating systems of especially small capacity are being developed and may be ready for use soon. Some combine, in a single equipment, two, three, four, or five different functions, relating to domestic hot water heating, space heating, air-to-air heat-exchanger operation, refrigeration, and summertime air cooling. Interesting developments lie close ahead.

Chapter 8
Performance

The performance of superinsulated houses can be summarized in a few sentences: In winter, even in a fairly cold location, the indoor temperature remains near 70°F and the cost of the auxiliary heat needed is close to negligible. Humidity is close to optimum. There is a steady supply of fresh air. In summer, even on long, hot sunny days, the indoor temperature rise is modest and a single ordinary-size air-conditioner may suffice. The incremental cost of superinsulation (cost of extra insulation, vapor barrier, air-to-air heat exchanger, minus the savings from having only a small auxiliary heating system) amounts to only a few percent of the overall cost of the house.

These conclusions apply to a wide range of latitude, a wide range of house-facing directions, and wide range of design styles.

Superinsulation is a real winner. It is here to stay.

The following sections are included for the benefit of architects and builders who are addicted to calculations. Ten years ago, when active and passive solar heating systems held the center of the stage, wide ranges of performance—good and bad—occurred. The houses could be much too cold in long cold cloudy spells, and big auxiliary heating systems were needed. The houses could become much too hot in long sunny spells, and there was need for much thermal mass, large attic vents, etc. There was a real need for detailed calculations, to avoid such troubles. Many experts spent years developing calculation methods and teaching others how to use them. Superb calculation methods are now available. But whether they are needed in thje designing of typical superinsulated houses is doubtful.

SOME BASIC TERMS

Some of the basic terms used in calculating building thermal performance are not as simple as they may at first appear. There are pitfalls, pointed out many years ago by G. S. Dutt, even to such simple terms as "winter," "average outdoor temperature in winter," and "degree-day value."

Winter

Smith and Jones live in the same town in New England. Smith, who lives in an uninsulated house, says that winter extends from September 1 to May 31. Throughout that period he makes much use of his furnace. Jones, who lives in a superinsulated house, says that winter extends from December 5 to March 15. He uses his furnace during that period only. To these two men, living in the same town, the term winter has very different meanings.

Average Outdoor Temperature in Winter

Smith, who uses his furnace from September 1 to May 31, says that the average outdoor temperature in winter is 45°F. Jones, who uses his furnace from December 5 to March 15, says that the average outdoor temperature in winter is 33°F. To these two men, the term average outdoor temperature in winter has very different meanings or values.

Microclimate

Another difficulty is that outdoor temperatures at locations only a few miles apart can differ greatly. On a cold windless night in winter the outdoor air near a house at the bottom of a valley may be 10°F colder than the air near a house at the top of the hill; cold air tends to go downward, and can fill a valley, while air at the hilltop may be warmer. On a sunny day in the summer the air near a house on a south slope may be much warmer than the air on a north slope, especially if there is no wind. For such reasons, average outdoor temperature near a particular house may differ considerably from thatd at a nearby weather station. (Such local differences are part of what is called microclimate, a concept too often overlooked.)

Degree-Day Value

The men who long ago defined degree-day and adopted 65°F as the base temperature have got heating engineers into a jam. All might have gone well if the decision had been made to use 70°F as a base (and to assume normal room temperature also to be 70°F), for then a degree-day value for any location would indicate straightforwardly the temperature deficiency, or shortfall in ourdoor temperature, relative to the desired indoor temperature.

Unfortunately, those men decided to throw in allowances for the typical amounts of intrinsic heating and direct-gain passive solar heating, assuming a typical amount of insulation in walls, ceilings, etc., and typical amounts of air leakage. At that time the inclusion of such allowances made fairly good sense inasmuch as most houses were more or less alike in those respects.

But today, houses differ widely in amounts of insulation, amounts of air leakage, and amounts of south-facing windows. Whereas 65°F may be a good choice of base temperature for Smith's house which has no insulation and few electrically powered devices, the best choice for Jones's house, which is superbly insulated and includes many kinds of electrically powered devices, might be 45°F.

Such differences in meanings of terms can play havoc with attempts to compare the performances of houses said to be situated in places that have the same degree-day values.

Some designers try to improve the situation by shifting the base used in calculating the degree-day value of a given location. But this is not easily done. In converting from base 65°F to, say, 45°F, no simple subtraction can suffice. Various reliable methods have been developed, but are outside the scope of this book.

CALCULATING HEAT LOSS: SOME DIFFICULTIES

Often a designer assumes for simplicity that the gross heat loss from a building is directly proportional to ΔT, the difference between indoor temperature, say 70°F, and outdoor temperature. Having made this assumption, he finds it reasonable to employ a standard, whole-winter degree-day figure, especially if he feels he can make a reasonably correct estimate of the pertinent base temperature (e.g., 65°F or 55°F) and can obtain the degree-day figure pertinent to this base.

Getting Wrong Results

Although roughly correct under various circumstances, the procedure described above sometimes leads to very wrong results, especially if the building is in a windy location, is several stories high, is very leaky, and has a large basement. Why does it give the wrong results?

1. It takes no account of changes in wind speed. The greater the speed, the greater the rate of in-leak of cold air and the rate of out-leak of warm air, that is, the greater the rate of heat-loss.

2. It takes no account of stack effect. This is the tendency (especially in a tall building) of cold air to leak into the lower part of the building and warm air to leak out of the upper part, even when there is no wind. The volume of in-leaking air increases with ΔT, and the heat-loss per unit of volume likewise increases with ΔT. Accordingly, the stack-effect heat loss is roughly proportional to the square of ΔT.

3. It takes no account of the fact that the basement may, typically, be much cooler than the rooms. On a day when the rooms are losing a moderate amount of heat, the basement may be losing none because it is at the same temperature as the outdoor air.

4. It takes no account of the fact that, in the first part of the winter, the basement, if cool, receives much heat from the underlying earth. The temperature of the earth a few feet below the basement is highest in the fall, not in midsummer, and lowest in the spring, not in midwinter! The basement-earth temperature cycle lags weeks or months behind the cycle of outdoor temperature.

Getting Better Results

Recognizing the foregoing complications, an engineer may use a more elaborate calculation: he may estimate the gross heat loss of the building by combining five terms:

Term proportional to ΔT.

Term proportional to $(\Delta T)^2$.

Term proportional to wind speed. (Note: If the house in question is in an exposed, windy location, heat-loss due to air leakage may be ten times greater than heat-loss due to stack-effect air leakage.)

Special term to correct for lag in basement-earth temperature.

Term for solar exposure.

VARIABILITY OF INTRINSIC HEAT

The intrinsic heat (from people, light bulbs, cooking stoves, etc.) varies greatly from hour to hour and also depends strongly on the lifestyles of the particular family occupying the house. Some families leave some windows partly open even in winter, keep a kitichen or bathroom exhaust fan running most of the time, and fail to close thermal shades at night. Other families do the opposite.

Again we must conclude that accurate predictions of thermal performance are not in the cards. It is best to settle for moderate accuracy, easily achieved with the aid of pocket calculators or low-cost computers.

CRITERIA OF THERMAL PERFORMANCE OF HOUSES EMPLOYING SOME PASSIVE SOLAR HEATING

Old Criteria

The following measures, or criteria, of thermal performance have been used extensively in judging houses that employ some passive solar heating:
- Total amount of useful heat provided by the solar heating system.
- Percent of needed heat provided by the solar heating system.
- Reduction in amount of auxiliary heat needed.
- Reduction in cost of fuel consumed.
- Solar Savings Fraction (SSF).
- Amount of auxiliary heat needed.

These criteria are moderately defective when applied to typical passively solar-heated houses—and even more defective when applied to superinsulated houses.

The first two criteria are poor because the solar heating system may create a large fraction of the heat need. Adding 200 sq ft of single-glazed south windows greatly increases the amount of solar radiation captured, but it also greatly increases the heat loss on a cold night. In some extreme cases the increase in heat need can exceed the increase in useful amount of solar energy collected. The result could be an increase in the amount of auxiliary heat needed!

The third and fourth criteria are fairly good, up to a point, but entirely overlook the important question, "Is a furnace still needed?" Saving a few hundred dollars in fuel costs is fine, but not as fine as saving a few thousand dollars on a big auxiliary heating system (furnace, chimney, oil tank, blower, ducts).

The fifth criterion, the Solar Savings Fraction, routinely used in the early 1980s, is doubly defective. It takes no account of whether the furnace can be eliminated, a major saving. Also, the method of choosing a comparison house (a prerequisite to computing the solar savings fraction) is vague and artificial.

It is vague in that the "solar aperture" is supposed to be (mentally) replaced with a panel that blocks all flow of energy, that is, transmits no solar radiation or other radiation and has no thermal conductance. (What, exactly, is a solar aperture? South windows? Southeast windows? East windows? North windows?)

It is artificial in that the resulting comparison structure, which in some cases is entirely dark and provides no view, is unlivable and therefore cannot properly be called a house. Worse yet, the structure consists of a mismatched combination of features: those specially chosen as parts of a solar house, and those squarely inappropriate, such as windows covered by energy-blocking panels. There seems to be little purpose in comparing an actual solar house with an artificial structure that is unlivable and includes a mismatched combination of solar and anti-solar features.

The last criterion is not fully relevant. It also takes no notice of savings from using a smaller auxiliary heating system. Such savings sometimes exceed the saving on fuel.

Better Criteria

The following criteria, phrased as questions, have greater validity, both for passive solar houses and for superinsulated houses.

What is the cost of the auxiliary heating system needed? For example, if only a single portable electric heater is needed, the cost may be insignificant. If a 70,000 Btu/hr oil furnace (with oil tank, chimney, heat distribution system, etc.) is needed, the cost may be highly significant: say $2,000 to $5,000.

What is the amount of auxiliary heat needed per year? If it is only two million Btu, or costs only a trivial amount, the owner of the house will be well pleased.

How uniform are the room temperatures throughout the daytime and evenings? Is the relative humidity satisfactory—between 35% and 55%, for example?

Are water-filled pipes safe from freezing even if in February supplies of heating fuel or electricity fail?

Does the house tend to remain cool in the summer? Or is it hard to keep cool? Some passive solar houses are disasters in summer.

Of course, durability, attractiveness and convenience are important. A house with a huge area of south windows may require movable insulation, and operating it may be a nuisance. (If the occupants are away, it may not be operated at all.)

Significant deprivations should be taken into account. A passively solar heated house that is largely underground may provide no view to east, north or west, and in summer may permit no through-draft from west to east (the direction of the prevailing wind). Also, it may provide very little privacy, if all rooms face a south terrace to which tradesmen or visitors have access.

If the thermal performance of a passively solar-heated house is to be compared with some other house, let the comparison be with the best superinsulated house of corresponding size.

Some passively solar-heated houses require enormous amount of auxiliary heat during a series of cold sunless days in February, while other may require little or no auxiliary heat at such times.

The expression fourth-day thermal vulnerability can be used to mean the amount of auxiliary heat needed to keep a house at 70°F in the fourth day of a many-day sunless period in February with typical temperatures. Only if this vulnerability is very small can the designer contemplate omitting a furnace or equivalent.

CRITERIA OF THERMAL PERFORMANCE

What performance criteria should be used in judging the behavior of a superinsulated house, if it has no furnace and requires practically no auxiliary heat because practically all of the heat needed is supplied intrinsically and by solar energy received via view windows of moderate area?

Main Criteria

The main criteria are (1) cost and durability of the house as a whole, (2) extent to which the air stays fresh, (3) extent to which temperature and humidity are within the comfort ranges, roughly 65 to 75°F and 30 to 60% relative humidity, and (4) general livability of the house, with attention paid to possible bonuses such as view in all four directions, wide range of view from each corner room, and attached sunspace or greenhouse. (An attached greenhouse may be a mixed blessing, producing not only vegetables and flowers but also bugs, unwanted moisture, and continual responsibility.)

The first criterion, cost of the house, is a reasonably definite concept. It can be estimated before construction and evaluated fairly accurately afterward. Durability may be hard to evaluate until the house has been in use many years. Air freshness is hard to define and measure in a general way, as is general liveability.

Auxiliary Heat Needed: Grand Performance Ratio

One can, obviously, simply state the annual amount of auxiliary heat needed. But such a statement is (a) dull, because the amount needed is so small if the house really is superinsulated, and (b) not very useful in comparing houses that are of different size or are located in different climates.

A measure coming into widespread use, in comparing the thermal performances of superinsulated houses, is annual auxiliary heat usage divided by the floor area of the heated portion of the house, and divided also by the annual degree-day value (relative to base 65°F) of the house site. The unit of measure is abbreviated as Btu/(ft2 dd). The quantity has had no name, but here the name "grand performance ratio" will be used. (The logic behind the measure is a little less than perfect, as explained in a later paragraph.)

The following table presents illustrative values of this ratio for a wide variety of house types.

GRAND PERFORMANCE RATIOS OF REPRESENTATIVE HOUSES

House	G P Ratio	House	G P Ratio
Leger house, prior to stopping last leaks and with no regular occupancy, four coldest months only.	2.5	Saskatchewan Conservation House with thermal shades in regular use.	0.6
Leger house for entire winter. No additonal auxiliary heat was needed in the additional months.	1.3	Average of 13 low-energy houses in Saskatchewan (1981).	2.0
		Lowest of 13 low-energy houses in Saskatchewan.	1.0
Leger house, but assuming normal occupancy and elimination of last air leaks.	0.9	"Typical house" as specified by Mid-American Solar Energy Complex.	12.5
Leger house, with addition of thermal shades.	0.4 to 0.6*	Goal adopted by Mid-American Solar Energy Complex: Solar 80 criterion.	2.5
Leger house, regarding warm basement as part of living area.	0.2 to 0.3*	Average of 100 superinsulated houses built in South Dakota in 1986.	2.5

*Casual guess; the exact values are of no importance provided they do not exceed 1.0 because the annual auxiliary heat cost is then negligible—less than the cost of dinner for eight persons at a good restaurant.

This ratio, the unit of which is Btu/(ft2 dd), is somewhat defective. It is now widely used, and comes close to being valid; yet it has shortcomings. The trouble is that it depends not only on the design of the house but also on climate, amount of solar radiation, local shading by buildings and trees, prevalence of wind, and manner in which the house is used.

Thermal climate. The amount of auxiliary heat needed in a superinsulated house is far from being proportional to the degree-day value if the usual 65°F base is used. (Using a different base won't work; different bases would be needed for houses insulated to different extents.). Also, even in locations with the same degree-day value, a given house may have very different grand performance ratio depending on how widely the temperature varies during the winter. If the range is narrow,the value might be 1; if large, it might be 2.

Solar radiation. A superinsulated house with very small window area may have almost the same grand performance ratio whether it is in a very sunny region or a cloudy region; but a house with a huge single-glazed south window area will perform very much better in a sunny region than in a cloudy region; even assuming that the regions have the same degree-day value, the grand performance ratio might be as different as 2 for the sunny region and 10 for the cloudy region.

Local shading. A given house may have a high or low grand performance ratio depending on whether the area to the south is clear or contains many tall buildings or tall trees.

Wind. The ratio may be high or low depending on the prevalence of high winds, especially if the house has little caulking or weatherstripping.

House use. To obtain a remarkably low ratio, the owner of the house could crowd in more occupants, reduce air-change rate from 0.5 to 0.25 changes per hour, encourage the frequent taking of showers and frequent use of the cooking stove and increased use of electric lights and appliances. Also, if the basement is warm, he could install a sofa there and include the basement area as part of the living area, which, if the house has only one story, doubles the living area and reduces the ratio by a factor of 2. None of these ploys are cheating; all are legitimate. But they greatly reduce the significance of house-to-house comparisons in terms of grand performance ratio.

Other Criteria

Gross heat loss. In a cold (7,500 degree-day) location a 1500 sq ft superinsulated house has a gross annual heat loss of from about 20 to 40 million Btu. Usually the amount is roughly proportional to the annual degree-day value. (Note: The value is of little importance, because most of the loss is made up by solar heat and by intrinsic heat sources. In other words, gross heat loss has little to do with the annual auxiliary heat need or the annual fuel cost.)

Rate of cool-down. Consider a typical superinsulated house situated in a cold climate, and consider a cold midwinter night when there is no intrinsic heat—say, the occupants are away and all utilities have been shut off. Under these extreme circumstances room temperature falls only very slowly—usually in the range of 0.3 to 1.0 Fahrenheit degrees per hour. Of course, ordinarily the house is occupied and various utilities are in use; the cool-down rate is then much lower. Such steadiness of temperature makes for comfort and also insures that, in a short period with all power supplies shut off, the house will remain livable for a long time without danger of water pipes' freezing.

PERFORMANCE IN SUMMER

In summer, superinsulated houses keep relatively cool—if the indoor heat production is kept at a minimum and if the windows and outside doors are kept closed during the day and are opened wide during the cool parts of the night. The thick insulation of the walls, roof, etc., keeps out heat during the day. The wide eaves shade the south windows. The east and west windows are not shaded, but they are quite small. It may pay to install awnings to shade them, or install special screens designed to block a large fraction of incident sunlight. Another strategy is to install a horizontal trellis close outside the windows.

In cooling a house at night, it may be worthwhile to employ a "whole-house" exhaust fan to drive out the old air and draw in new. In an article in Alternative Sources of Energy (41, Jan-Feb 1980), S. Baer explained the desirability of maintaining a large flow of incoming cool air at night—so that the rate at which the walls typically give off heat to the room air will be matched by the rate at which the room-air heat can be driven outdoors.

Effectiveness of Eaves

How effective are eaves in excluding solar radiation at south windows in summer? They are much less effective than one might assume. Typically, they cut the amount of solar radiation entering south windows by only about 50%, according to an article by Utzinger and Klein in Solar Age (23, 1979, p. 369).

Why is this? Because of the importance of the diffuse component of solar radiation and also radiation that is reflected from the ground. Against them, the eaves have little effect. Even direct solar radiation fails to be blocked by the eaves at times far from noon; at 9 a.m., for example, the sun is low enough in the sky so that the rays pass beneath the eaves and reach the south windows; and the same is true of 3 p.m. radiation. If the house aims 20 or 30 degrees off-south, the eaves are even less effective.

Windows on the east and west sides of the house receive almost no benefit from eaves—because direct solar radiation reaches these windows only when the sun is low in the sky. Awnings can be helpful here, as can external shutters.

Of course, if the designer somehow arranges to block more than (say) 60% of the solar radiation reaching east, south, and west windows in summer, the threat of overheating of the rooms is so small that a somewhat greater window area may be chosen.

CONDENSATION ON WINDOWS

Recent tests have shown that well-insulated windows are helpful as regards discouraging the condensation of water. A shift from ordinary glass to low-e glass causes the inner glass sheets to be sufficiently warmer that room-air relative humidity can be as much as 8 percentage points higher before any water will condense on the windows. Thus comfortably high relative humidity can be maintained—without risk of condensation—even in extremely cold weather. (Source: Air Infiltration Review, Feb 1987, p. 7.)

COMPUTER PROGRAMS AVAILABLE
TO ANALYZE THERMAL PERFORMANCE

Computers have become a big boon to house designers. Using a moderately priced microcomputer, a designer, architect, or builder can calculate fairly accurately (within about 10%, typically) the main facts on thermal performance of a proposed house of almost any size, style, etc., in almost any climate in the USA or Canada. In particular, he can calculate:

The maximum amount of auxiliary heat needed in the coldest hour of the winter. Such information permits the designer to decide the necessary capacity, or heat output rating, of the oil or gas furnace, or electric heater, or other source of auxiliary heat. He can specify the size that is fully adequate to the peak heat need, yet is not oversized (an oversized heater takes up more space, costs more, runs less efficiently, and provides uneven heating).

The amount of auxiliary heat needed in the winter as a whole—and the cost of this heat, whether it be supplied by oil, gas, electricity, or other means.

The maximum amount of cooling needed during the hottest hour of summer. Knowing this, the designer can choose a cooling system that is just the right size.

The amount of cooling needed in the summer as a whole—and its cost.

The procedure is simple. The computer, employing a disk on which the calculation program is recorded, displays on a screen sets and subsets ("menus") of questions: for example, questions as to the number, size and type of windows of each room, the directions in which the windows face, and the width of eaves that shade the windows from the sun.

Equally detailed questions are presented as to the structures of the walls, ceilings, roof, basement walls, external doors, etc., the air-tightness of the house, and the rate of forced intake of fresh air.

And there are questions also about the location of the house: knowing the location, the computer itself supplies standard detailed information on outdoor temperature, sunshine, etc.

When all the design information has been fed into the computer, a key is pressed and in seconds the computer presents the answers on the screen. Note that the computer operator does not need to know any engineering or mathematics; he simple feeds in the design facts, presses a key, and receives the answers as to peak heat need, annual heat need, annual heat cost—and the same for summer cooling.

Better yet, the designer can propose some attractive-seeming design change—for example, replacing double-glazed windows with triple-glazed windows—and find out, almost at once, how this affects the overall performance. By "quizzing" the computer on many small design-change options, he can optimize the design.

How does one get hold of these almost miraculous computer programs? They are now widely available among engineering and architectural firms, and are used routinely on projects for clients. They can be obtained also from the program originators and from various distributing agencies. Some of the main sources are listed in the following section.

SOURCES OF THERMAL ANALYSIS COMPUTER PROGRAMS

Air Conditioning Contractors of America, 1228 17 St NW, Washington DC 20036. Telephone: (202) 296 7610. This association distributes a $300 program called RIGHT-J for use with IBM PCs and its compatibles. It takes into account hundreds of details of building design, and gives almost instant answers to the peak heat need in winter and peak cooling need in summer. Hundreds of contractors and architects throughout USA have purchased and use this program. The program can be obtained also from the engineering firm that created it:

Wright Associates, Inc., 15 Blueberry Lane, Lexington MA 02173. Telephone: (617) 862-8719.

Harold Orr and Associates, 1317 Wilson Crescent, Saskatoon, Saskatchewan, Canada S7J 3J8. Telephone: (306) 343 9733. In recent years Orr and colleagues, working at the National Research Council of Canada, have developed highly sophisticated programs specifically for designers of superinsulated houses. The latest program, called HOTCAN 3 or HOTCAN 2000, is especially accurate. It costs about $100 US.

HOTCAN 3 is also available from Energy Analysis Software, PO Box 7081, Postal Station J, Ottawa, Canada K2A 3Z6. Price about $149 Canadian.

Burt Hill Kosar Rittelmann Associates, 400 Morgan Center, Butler PA 16001. Supplies, for about $400, a versatile program, EEDO.

Energy Toolworks, 207 Kent Ave. #1, Kentfield, CA 94904. Supplies MICROPAS programs priced at about $200 to $300.

Enercomp, 757 Russell Blvd., Suite A3, Davis, CA 95616. Telephone: (916) 753 3400. Supplies a very sophisticated program, MICROPAS 2.0, for about $800.

F-Chart Software, 4406 Fox Bluff Rd., Middleton, WI 53562. Sells the F-LOAD program for building energy analysis, for major types of microcomputers, for $425.

John Wiley & Sons, Inc., 605 Third Ave., New York, NY 10158. Sells, for about $400, a program "Passive Solar Design" developed by Cornerstones Energy Group, Inc.

LAWRENCE BERKELEY LABORATORY REPORTS ON PERFORMANCE

A tremendous job has been done by the Lawrence Berkeley Laboratory in examining and appraising energy efficient buildings throughout the USA and writing reports on every aspect of building performance. Most of the reports are free and are available from the Energy Performance of Buildings Group of the Applied Science Division, Bldg. 90, Lawrence Berkeley Laboratory, University of California, Berkeley, CA 94720.

GENERAL CONCLUSIONS AND PROSPECTS FOR THE FUTURE

Superinsulation is here to stay. It is a sure-fire winner, with its even temperature, favorable humidity, low heating cost, steady fresh air supply and also its tendency to keep the house cool in summer. The annual heating bill is almost negligible. Cost of construction is only a few percent greater than that of conventional houses. The limitations of actively solar heated houses are avoided, and likewise the limitations of passive solar heating.

Superinsulation offers bonuses to architects, builders, and bankers also. Architects like it because it is so tolerant of house orientation, shading, and cold overcast weather and because no very elaborate calculations of solar inputs and added thermal mass are needed. Bulders like it because no strange huge window-walls are involved, no special floors or vents; for the most part the materials and construction methods are the old familiar ones. Bankers who supply the mortgage money like it because they know that the home-owners will have very low heating bills and so will be in good position to make their payments on time; accordingly the bankers may be inclined to allow greater mortgage amounts, permitting the potential buyer to choose a house of slightly greater size or better quality. Realtors like it because houses of this type, with their high comfort and low heating bills, are easy to sell.

Are further refinements of design in the offing? Yes. More is being learned year by year about vapor barriers and air-and-water barriers and the best ways of installing them. Better air-to-air heat-exchangers are becoming available; efficiency is being increased, defrosting is being simplified, and costs may decrease. Several groups are working on combination systems that will combine, perhaps in a single package, the functions of ventilation, fresh air supply, heat recovery, domestic hot water heating, auxiliary heat supply, and summertime cooling. Windows with much higher R-values, perhaps as high as 5 to 8, may become widely available. Strategies for accommodating sunspaces and greenhouses are being improved.

But there is no need to wait for such refinements. Superinsulation is already a mature and well proven technology.

Chapter 9

Retrofit Insulation

Almost any poorly insulated house can be brought up to superinsulation standards. Comfort is increased and heating bills are drastically reduced. But the cost is high; a great variety of tasks are involved and require much care in planning and execution.

Several basic strategies are available. The choice depends on type of house, conditions of outer walls' interior and exterior faces, local contractors' skills, local building codes, and many other factors. The choice depends also on whether the family intends to continue living in the house during the many months of retrofit work and whether budget limitations will force the use of short-cuts and compromises.

The cost of the retrofit superinsulation can be reduced if the work is done as part of a general remodeling; much of the work of adding insulation and improving airtightness can then be done without large extra effort. Conversely if superinsulation work is to be done, upgrading of wiring, plumbing, heating, etc., can be done at the same time relatively economically.

Before retrofit superinsulation can be started, this big quesiton must be answered: Is the additional insulation to be applied to the outer walls' interior faces or exterior faces? The respective merits of these two options are discussed in the following sections. In some cases it may be necessary to use a mix of strategies: modify some walls (those facing the street, for example) on the interior, to retain setback or appearance, while modifying other walls on the exterior. Such a mix poses special difficulties in vapor barrier installation, but these can be overcome by thoughtful design and careful construction.

Choice of Interior Retrofit

An interior retrofit is the usual choice by a homeowner who lacks the money or spare time needed to complete the project within a few months. Working in the interior, he can proceed room by room at his own pace as time and money permit. This choice makes especially good sense, if:

• The house can be emptied of people and furniture; the work can then be done without regard to how much dust, noise, and general confusion are produced.
• The walls' interior faces are in poor condition and must be rebuilt or refinished in any event.
• The walls contain wiring or plumbing that is obsolete and must be replaced.
• The rooms are large enough so that thickening the wall on the inside will not reduce room size noticeably.
• Much rain, snow, wind, or extreme cold is expected.
• The persons who will do the work dislike climbing ladders.
• Local regulations prohibit changing the exteriors of houses of historic importance, and the house in question has been declared to be such a house.

Choice of Exterior Retrofit

An exterior retrofit is the best choice if the homeowner wants the job to be finished quickly and can affort to hire a competent contractor. Working on the house exterior, the contractor finds the project to be relatively straightforward; in favorable cases the work can be completed within a few weeks. This choice makes especially good sense, if:

- The family insists on remaining in the house while the work is being done.
- The exterior faces of the walls are in poor condition and must be rebuilt in any event.
- The rooms are so small that further encroachment cannot be permitted.
- Shrubs, trees, and nearby buildings do not limit access.
- An addition is planned and a unified external appearance is desired.
- Local regulations cause no problems.

COST AND SAVING

Obviously the cost of retrofit superinsulation will depend on so many circumstances that no one figure can apply generally. Often the cost may be in the range $8 to $15 per square foot of floor area, which may be equivalent to 1/6 to 1/3 of the cost of a brand new superinsulated house. Costs may be greater yet if, on opening up the walls, the contractor finds rotted sills or other unexpected horrors.

Cost will be much less if the owner himself does most of the work. But he would do well to think hard before undertaking this: has he the necessary skills, proper tools, and physical endurance? Does he know how to work safely? Is he prepared to give up evening and weekend pleasures to the long hard retrofit work? Can his wife and children stand the strain? Has he estimated realistically the time required—months, or in some cases, years?

The rewards, of course, are great: a big increase in comfort, and 70 to 90% reduction in amount of auxiliary heat needed. If the job is done well and the appearance of the house, inside and out, is excellent, the resale value of the house may be enormously increased.

The change in cash flow will benefit the community. Money that formerly went to a distant oil producer or distant utility will benefit, instead, local contractor personnel, local lumber supply centers, etc. If thousands of homeowners superinsulate their existing houses, the electric utilities will find their peak electric loads reduced and may conclude that proposed new billion-dollar plants are not needed.

Often the cost of the retrofit is handled by obtaining a loan from a bank. Bankers, recognizing that owners of superinsulated houses have lower heating bills and thus find it easier to make monthly payments on mortgages and loans, look favorably on requests for loans to cover costs of superinsulation.

GENERAL PLAN OF ACTION

The main steps in retrofit insulation include:
- Including additional insulation in the walls, ceilings or roof, and basement; add enough to provide a thermal resistance of R-20 to R-60, depending on how cold the climate is.
- Including, in all outside walls and in roofs or ceilings, a continuous vapor barrier; usually a 0.006-inch-thick film of ultra-violet-protected polyethylene is used.
- Converting single-glazed or double-glazed windows to triple or quadruple glazing.
- Widening all window sills, window jambs, and exterior door jambs to accommodate the increase in wall thickness.

- Caulking large and small cracks, sealing holes, and thus making the house reasonably airtight—tight enough so that, on a typical day in winter, less that about 1/4 house-volume of old air leaks out each hour.
- Installing equipment (an air-to-air heat-exchanger) capable of expelling from the house 1/2 of a house-volume of air each hour and causing intake of an equal amount of fresh air. In other words, providing for about 1/2 air-change per hour—to eliminate harmful or smelly gases and bring in a generous amount of fresh air,
- Relocating wiring and plumbing as may be required.

Books Giving Detailed Instructions

Detailed instructions as to how to perform retrofit superinsulation are outside the scope of this book. Different instructions are required for different types of existing houses—wood-frame houses, brick houses, stucco houses, etc., also one-story houses, two-story houses, etc., also houses with basement or crawl space. Such instructions can easily fill a thick book.

Fortunately, such books are available. Especially valuable are the ones listed below. (For details as to publisher, price, etc., see Bibliography.)

Marshall and Argue, *The Superinsulated Retrofit Book.*

Nisson and Dutt, *The Superinsulated Home Book.*

Orr and Dumont, *A Major Energy Conservation Retrofit of a Bungalow.*

Chapter 10
Air-to-Air Heat Exchangers

Interest in air-to-air heat-exchangers is increasing by leaps and bounds. As recently as 1980 many architects and builders had never heard of them. Yet today practically all architects and builders (and many homeowners also) recognize the need for them in tightly built houses, and are anxious to learn more about their peformance and cost.

The surge of interest may be explained by these facts:

1. Our understanding of indoor pollutants and the health threats they pose has increased. New kinds of pollutants have appeared on the scene. For example, formaldehyde compounds contained in particleboard and radon gas from the earth. Today's new houses are much tighter than houses built decades ago. Infiltration rates have been reduced by factors of 3 to 10. Result: concentrations of pollutants can build up to dangerous levels.

2. Because the house loses little heat and the furnace runs only occasionally, furnace-induced air change is minimal.

3. Because the houses are so tight and infiltration rates are so low, the humidity of the indoor air can build up excessively, resulting in condensation on windows and other cold surfaces.

4. The threat of indoor pollution is being publicized in the popular press. Countless articles in newspapers and magazines have alerted the public to the very real dangers.

The central question is: How can the occupants of a superinsulated house provide a steady inflow of fresh air and steady outflow of stale air without losing an enormous amount of heat and incurring a whopping heating bill?

The answer, of course, is to (1) steer clear of building materials and furnishings that are pollutant-rich, and (2) use an air-to-air heat-exchanger. The exchanger does its job well, may cost only $350 to $1,000, and may have an annual operating cost of only $40 to $100.

The need for air-to-air heat-exchangers is now widely recognized by architects, public health experts, and government agencies concerned with housing. Among the first agencies to recognize the importance of such exchangers was the provincial government of Saskatchewan. On June 1, 1981, it established a formal requirement that, if the owner of a new energy-efficient house was to qualify for an interest-free loan and if the house was to have a forced-air type of heating system, this system "... must be designed in such a way that an air-to-air heat-exchanger can be added to the system at a later date, if it is found advisable by the occupant ... ."

DEFINITION

Any device that removes (extracts, recovers, salvages) heat from one airstream and delivers it to another airstream is called an air-to-air heat exchanger.

Many such exchangers are employed in industries that produce large volumes of warm and highly polluted air. Such devices may be large, heavy, and expensive. Many were designed and built many decades ago and are still in use today.

What is new is the development of small, lightweight, inexpensive exchangers meant solely for use in tightly built houses. Most of the 25 or 30 types now commercially available were designed within the last few years; the designs are being improved steadily, and persons who write articles on these devices are kept busy keeping up with new developments. Air-to-air heat-exchangers are often referred to by other names, such as recuperators, regenerators, and heat-recovery-ventilation (HRV) units. But the name "air-to-air heat-exchanger" seems especially simple and clear.

TWO KINDS OF HEAT

Sensible Heat and Latent Heat

Ordinary room air contains heat of two kinds: sensible and latent. Familiarity with these two kinds of heat is important, especially as air-to-air heat-exchangers treat the two kinds differently. All of the exchangers recover sensible heat, but some recover very little latent heat.

Sensible heat is heat that can be sensed by your fingertip or by a thermometer. It is the most common type of heat.

Latent heat is heat that has converted a solid into a liquid or has converted a liquid to a gas. It takes much heat to melt a block of ice, even if the resulting water is just as cold as the ice and your fingertip fails to find any increase in temperature. Likewise it takes much heat to boil away a gallon of water, even if the resulting steam is no hotter than the boiling water.

Amounts of Sensible Heat and Latent Heat in Room Air

If room air contained just pure air—no water vapor at all—we could forget about latent heat. The changes involved in heating or cooling the air would involve sensible heat only. But in fact room air contains, typically, 1/2 to 2 percent of water vapor (gaseous H_2O molecules) and this small-seeming amount contains an impressively large amount of latent heat. An easy way to show the importance of such latent heat is to point out that to raise the temperature of a pound of water 1 degree requires only one Btu (British thermal unit) of energy, but to convert 1 pound of boiling water to steam requires 1,054 Btu—roughly a thousand-fold difference!

Which Type of Heat Does an Air-to-Air Heat-Exchanger Recover?

Many exchangers can recover both. However, most of the heat recovered is of sensible type. In spring, summer, and fall the outdoor air is not extremely cold, and therefore it does not drastically chill the outgoing stale air and does not cause any condensation of gaseous water to liquid water. Thus there is no change in latent heat; latent heat plays no role and does not need to be considered at all.

But in midwinter the situation is very different. The outdoor air is very cold, and it cools the outgoing stale air so drastically that most of its water content changes from gas to liquid or—in extreme cases—to solid. The result is a large release of latent heat, and much of this can assist in the warming of the incoming fresh air.

Thus designers of air-to-air heat-exchanger have to take both kinds of heat into account if the efficiency of heat recovery is to be high. Several very different strategies, discussed in a later chapter, are available.

Two Embarrassments: Production of Water and Ice

It is an embarrassment to exchanger designers that when moisture in the outgoing stale air is condensed, the equipment may steadily drip water. It is essential that the water find its way to a drain spout and that a tube be provided to carry the water to a house drain. Otherwise a large puddle of water would form. So: good drainage is an ingredient of all exchangers.

A much worse embarrassment is that, in very cold weather, the condensate will freeze and form ice, and the amount of ice tends to increase until it completely blocks the passageways for outgoing air and stops the airflow here. Designers have given great effort to finding schemes for avoiding build-up of ice. Several strategies are available; some require occupant attention every day or every few hours; others are fully automatic. Every year, better "defrosting" schemes become available.

Humidity: Absolute and Relative

There are two measures (two kinds) of humidity: absolute humidity and relative humidity. Absolute humidity means the actual absolute amount of H_2O in a pound of air and is expressed in pounds of water per pound of dry air. Relative humidity is the ratio of (a) actual amount of water contained in the given body of air to (b) the greatest amount of water that this air, at its given temperature, can hold. (If you try to make it hold more, you will find that "rain" begins to fall.) The ratio, called RH, is usually expressed as a percentage.

PROPERTIES OF AIR

Dry air at standard atmospheric pressure consists of 78.1% (by volume) nitrogen, 21.0% oxygen, and 0.9% of other gases.

The density of ordinary sea-level air at various temperatures—and at sea-level atmospheric pressure—is shown in the following table. Also shown are the specific volume, specific heat at constant pressure, and viscosity. (Viscosity is sometimes called absolute viscosity, or dynamic viscosity. A somewhat different concept—not used in this book   is kinematic viscosity; it is the ordinary, or absolute, viscosity divided by the density of the gas or liquid in question.)

SOME PROPERTIES OF AIR (AT SEA LEVEL)

Temperature (°F)	lb mass per ft^3	Density (lb force)(sec2) / (ft^4)	Specific volume (ft^3/lb)	Specific heat at constant pressure (Btu)/(lb °F)	Viscosity (lb force)(sec) / (ft^2)
25 to 35	0.081	0.0025	12.3	0.24	3.6×10^{-7}
55 to 65	0.075	0.0023	13.3	0.24	3.7×10^{-7}
70	0.074*	0.0023	13.6	0.24	3.8×10^{-7}
95 to 105	0.070	0.0022	14.2	0.24	4.0×10^{-7}

*Some authors use 0.077. I do too, sometimes (inconsistently!). Source: McAdams, p. 411.

Sample Use of Table

Question 1: How much heat is needed to raise the temperature of one pound of 69°F air to 70°F? Answer: Inspection of the table shows the answer to be 0.24 Btu.

Question 2: How much heat is needed to raise the temperature of one cubic foot of air at 69°F (and at standard pressure) to 70°F? Answer: (0.077 lb)(0.24 Btu/lb) = 0.0185 Btu.

Question 3: How much heat is needed to raise the temperature of one cubic foot of air from 30°F to 70°F? Answer: 40 x 0.0185 Btu = 0.74 Btu. (Here I neglect the fact that 30°F air is slightly denser than 70°F air.)

Question 4: How much heat is needed to raise the temperature of 10,000 ft^3 of air (about one typical houseful) from 30°F to 70°F? Answer: About 10,000 x 0.74 Btu = 7400 Btu.

The specific heat of air changes very little with temperature: Less than one part in a thousand for the range from 0°F to 70°F.

COMPUTING THE MOISTURE CONTENT OF AIR

Problems involving the moisture content of air are easily solved with the aid of a special graph called the *psychrometric chart*. It shows you at a glance how the moisture content depends on temperature and relative humidity; in fact it shows the relationships between four key quantities: temperature, relative humidity, absolute humidity, and energy (enthalpy). Knowing any two of these quantities, you can find the other two—instantly.

The horizontal axis of the chart is temperature—simply the temperature of whatever air is under discussion. At the left are low temperatures, at the right are high temperatures.

The vertical axis is the absolute amount of water (gaseous H_2O) in the air. Zero content is at the bottom of the graph. Marks along the vertical axis indicate water content in terms of "pounds of water per pound of dry air."

The heavy sloping curved line at the left marks the boundary of possible moisture content. For example, the greatest amount of moisture that a pound of 32°F air can hold is about 0.004 pounds, that is, about 0.4%. The amount increases ever more steeply with increasing temperature, which explains why the curved line becomes ever steeper as one deals with higher and higher temperatures.

The lowest of the curved lines shows how much moisture is being held by a body of air if the amount of moisture is just one tenth of the maximum amount. This line is called the "10% relative humidity" curve.

The middle curve refers to air that contains 50% of the maximum possible amount of moisture. It is called the "50% relative humidity" curve. In all, ten curved lines are shown; they are called the 10%, 20%, 30%, 40%, 50%, 60%, 70%, 80%, 90% and 100% relative humidity curves.

Example: How much water is contained in 70°F air that has a relative humidity of 50%? To find the answer, one finds where the vertical line at 70°F intersects the "50% relative humidity" curve, and one then finds the "same height" point on the vertical scale at the right. This point is seen to correspond to about 0.77%. That is, 100 pounds of 70°F 50% RH air contains about 0.77 lb of gaseous water.

Examples of use of enthalpy scale:

To convert 1 lb of air from A to B (i.e., to heat the air without changing its absolute humidity) requires, as reference to the enthalpy scale shows, the addition of about 17 Btu.

To convert from B to C (i.e., to increase the absolute humidity while keeping the temperature constant) requires about 17 Btu. (Same amount—by coincidence).

To convert from C to D requires no enthalpy. The gain in sensible heat just equals the loss in latent heat.

PSYCHROMETRIC CHART
Multipurpose humidity graphs pertinent to air at standard pressure

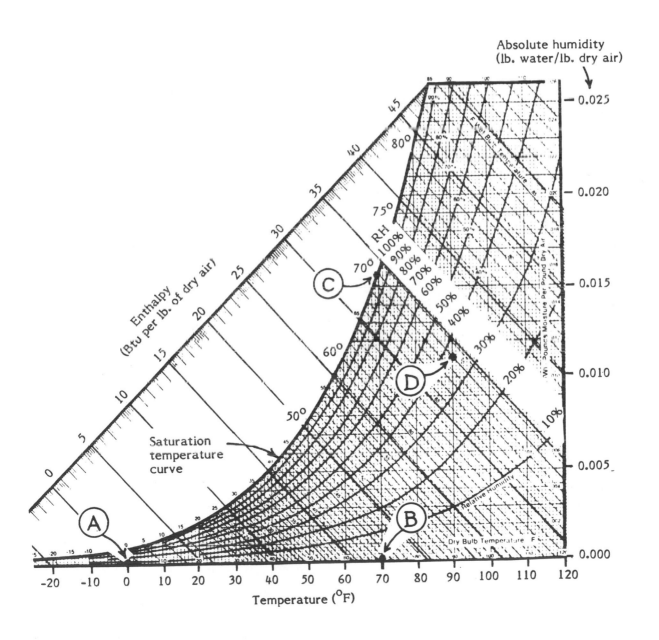

Warning

Typical presentations of psychrometric charts have been slightly "fudged." If one wishes to be strictly accurate in preparing such a chart, one can arrange for *no more than two* parameters to conform to straight and uniformly spaced lines. Often, however, the draftsman shows additional sets of straight and uniformly spaced lines; this makes his task easier and makes the graph easier for persons to understand. The price paid is a very small sacrifice in accuracy (all as explained in Bibliography; see item S-162).

Note: The chart contains *two* sets of lines that slope upward to the left: set of guidelines pertinent to the enthalpy scale (lines of constant enthalpy), and set of constant wet-bulb-temperature lines. Lines of the former set are straight and parallel. Lines of the latter set are not quite straight and not quite parallel. All of which may produce some "visual confusion."

The chart has one more valuable capability: it can show you, at once, the total amount of heat (sensible and latent—a sum called "enthalpy") of air of any given temperature and moisture content. One simply finds the corresponding point on the sloping scale at the upper left (enthalpy scale, reading directly in Btu per pound of air). In finding the corresponding point one must "travel" along the straight guidelines that run upward to the left.

Example: How much more energy (enthalpy) does a pound of 70°F, 50% RH air contain than a pound of 0°F, 0% RH contains? Find the intersection point of the 70°F vertical line and 50% RH curved line, then look upward to the left and arrive at the point corresponding to about 26 Btu/lb. Proceeding similarly for 0°F, 0% RH, one finds the enthalpy value to be 0 Btu/hr. (This is no coincidence; the originators of the chart took 0°F, 0% RH air as the base of the scale; they chose it as the arbitrary embodiment of zero enthalpy.) (Note: Energy must always be specified relative to an arbitrary base. There is no obvious absolute base.) Thus the answer is 26 minus 0, or 26 Btu/lb.

NEEDED: A STEADY FORCED SUPPLY OF FRESH AIR

An air-to-air heat-exchanger provides a steady supply of fresh air. The flow continues at the same rate irrespective of windspeed and chimney effect. The rate of supply can be set at optimum value—optimum with respect to control of noxious gases and also humidity, and the rate will hold steady.

(Norman Saunders, Weston MA designer, has proposed that when the outdoor temperature is very low, making chimney effect large, the controls of an air-to-air heat-exchanger should ideally slightly reduce the blower speeds. Perhaps it should be reduced further when wind speed is high. If such a control system were used, the *combined* rate of fresh air intake—natural and forced— could be held approximately constant and there would be some saving on electrical power used.)

ALTERNATIVE GOALS OF AIR-TO-AIR HEAT EXCHANGER USE

In operating an air-to-air heat-exchanger, a homeowner may have either of two different goals, depending on whether the room-air humidity is just right or too high.

If the room-air humidity is just right, indicated by Point A in the accompanying left diagram, the exchanger should ideally merely swap properties of the outgoing stale room air and the incoming fresh air (Point B). That is, ideally, the temperature and humidity of the stale air should be transferred to the incoming air, and the temperature and humidity of the incoming air should be transferred to the outgoing stale air. Thus the house would receive fresh air and there would be no change in indoor temperature or humidity. Ideal!

The arrows in the central diagram suggest the transfers from stale air and from fresh air. For an ideal exchanger of this type, the arrows slope equally and oppositely and are equal in length.

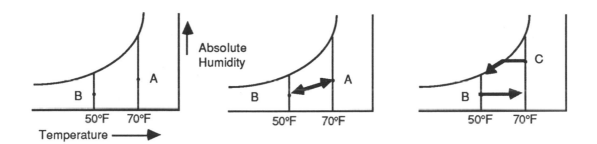

If the room air is too humid (Point C in diagram at right), the exchanger should ideally swap temperatures of the outgoing air and incoming air but should not swap moisture: there should be a net outflow of moisture. The arrows of the diagram at the right show a suitable exchange.

As explained in a later chapter, actual exchangers can approximate either of these goals but not both. A buyer must choose between an exchanger that always exchanges temperature and moisture and an exchanger that exchanges temperature only. The writer has invented (on paper!) a two-mode exchanger that can provide both kinds of performance; but such a device does not exist and in any case would be more complicated and more costly.

NATURAL INFILTRATION IS NOT A SOLUTION

The causes and mechanisms of natural infiltration are discussed in Chap. 6.

What is the typical rate of inflow of fresh air via infiltration? According to rumor, the rate for typical houses that are at least 10 or 20 years old is about 1 to 10 house volumes per hour, depending on the size of the house, the type of construction (wood? brick? concrete?), care used in construction, type of sheathing used, condition of windows and doors, extent to which the house is exposed to high winds, and various habits of the occupants. For houses 5 to 10 years old, the rate is usually lower: say 1/2 to 2 house volumes per hour. For houses being built today by contractors concerned about saving energy, the rate is probably even lower: about 1/3 to 2 house volumes per hour. For certain very carefully built superinsulated houses, the rate may be 1/20 to 1/3 house volume per hour.

The rates are seldom known—seldom known even roughly.

In any event, it is usually true that *no single number* can be satisfactory—partly because the rate changes from day to day and hour to hour, and partly because each room may have a different rate (especially if doors between rooms are kept shut).

It seems deplorable that so many architects and engineers ignore these facts—they often speak as though a given house had a definite rate of natural infiltration, such as "... one air change per hour," when, in fact, the rate can be anywhere from 0 to 5, say, depending on outdoor temperature and windspeed. The variations are important! They may imply serious hazard to health, and they certainly imply occasional enormous waste of heat.

Clearly, to rely on natural infiltration is ill-advised. The rate of infiltration will sometimes be much too high, implying big waste on heat and big heating bills, and at other times may be too low, leading to discomfort and risk to health.

Sources of Information on Infiltration

The latest information on the causes and control of infiltration is made available routinely in *Air Infiltration Review* (published by the Air Infiltration and Ventilation Center, Old Bracknell Lane, Bracknell, Berkshire, Great Britain RG 12 4AH.) See also the periodicals listed in the Bibliography of this book.

AIR-CLEANING DEVICES ARE NOT SOLUTIONS

To make the needed improvements in indoor air quality, why not simply install an electrical air-cleaning device designed to collect and remove particulate matter? For example, why not use the Air Care ionizing and collecting device marketed by Dev Industries, Inc. 5721 Arapahoe Avenue, Boulder CO 80303?—or the Modulion device sold by Life Energy Products Inc., P.O. Box 75, G.P.O., Brooklyn NY 11202? Because most such devices (1) are mainly effective with respect to actual particles, whereas a large fraction of room pollutants are gases, (2) do not get rid of excessive moisture, carbon dioxide, radon, etc., and (3) do not replenish the supply of oxygen.

A SIMPLE EXHAUST FAN IS SELDOM A GOOD SOLUTION

Some builders have turned their backs on air-to-air heat-exchangers, claiming that these devices have too many drawbacks: need for extensive ductwork, need for drain, defrosting problems, and high cost.

These builders employ, instead, one or more simple exhaust fans: an exhaust fan in the kitchen, perhaps another in the bathroom, and perhaps others also. Such fans expel the stale air and, because of the result depressurization of the house, produce a corresponding inflow of fresh air. The inflow may occur informally at various locations (cracks, etc.); or a special inlet port may be provided and an electrical heater can be installed here so that the incoming air will not chill the occupants. (This approach has been described clearly by Steve Loken in the Feb. 1987 issue of *Progressive Builder*.)

This strategy, although successful in various simple situations, is often unsatisfactory:

• There is much waste of heat. No heat is recovered from the outgoing air.
• If the incoming fresh air enters at many locations, there is no easy way of preheating it. It may chill the occupants.
• If this air enters at a single location and is heated by an electrical heater, the cost of the electricity may be high.
• The fan slightly depressurizes the house and, in extreme cases, could cause back-drafting, that is, could suck within-chimney air downward and into the rooms, contaminating room air with noxious fumes. (The threat is absent if the house contains no chimney—no furnace, no wood

stove, etc.—or if such devices are present but have tightly fitted ducts that supply combustion air directly from outdoors.)

A humorous remark overheard at a meeting of exchanger manufacturers was, "I like to say that what I am selling is a simple exhaust fan plus a gadget that warms the incoming air, insures that there will be no depressurization, and has especially low annual operating cost. My exchangers perform all these functions."

One of the main components of the cost of an air-to-air heat-exchanger may be the cost of the ductwork needed to insure good air quality in all principal parts of the house. Exchanger manufacturers point out that this cost should not be charged against the exchanger, since proper ductwork may be needed even when an exhaust-only system is used.

Chapter 11

Radon: An Insidious Pollutant

INTRODUCTION

Radon—a radioactive gas that seeps up from the ground—is of little or no importance in most parts of America. Yet in a few parts, depending on the nature of the underlying minerals, it is a serious hazard to health. Therefore it deserves detailed discussion in this book.

Readers living in regions that are free of radon should skip this chapter.

Persons having an in-depth interest in radon may wish to consult the following excellent books:

Radiation Protection, by Prof. Jacob Shapiro of the Harvard School of Public Health. Published in 1981 by the Harvard University Press, Cambridge MA 02138. 500 pp. $25.

Radiation and Human Health, by Dr. J. W. Gofman. Published in 1981 by Sierra Club Books, 530 Bush Street, San Francisco CA 94108. 910 pp. $30.

Indoor Pollutants, by the National Academy of Sciences, Committee on Indoor Pollutants. Published in 1981 by National Academy Press, 2101 Constitution Avenue, Washington DC 20418. ISBN 0-309-03188-5. 560 pp. $16.25. An authoritative book.

Pamphlets issued by the US Environmental Protection Agency in 1986 and 1987, which are extremely helpful, are listed near the end of this chapter.

RADON: WHAT IS IT?

Radon is one of the 92 naturally occurring elements. It is one of the heaviest ones. The radon nucleus contains 86 protons, and accordingly radon has been assigned the atomic number 86. It is called $_{86}$Rn.

Radon contains a much larger number of neutrons: about 134 of them. The naturally occurring radon nuclei contain 133, 134, or 136 of them. Thus the *total* number of particles (total number of nucleons) in such nucleus is 219, 220, or 222. These three types (three isotopes, or nuclides) are called ^{219}Rn, ^{220}Rn, and ^{222}Rn.

Every radon atom has an enveloping cloud, or set of shells, of electrons. The outermost shell is of special type, called full, or *closed*, and accordingly the atom has practically no external electrical effects (as long as the nucleus remains quiescent!). It ignores all other atoms of every type whatsoever, and exists in splendid isolation, i.e., as a monatomic chemically inert gas ("noble gas").

Radon nuclei are unstable. Eventually every such nucleus disintegrates, or "explodes." There is no known way to prevent this and no known way to control or predict when the disintegration of any given atom will occur.

Consequently if you have in your house a large quantity of radon atoms—say a billion of them—you will find that, every little while (at random times) one atom will disintegrate. Thus radon is said to be radioactive.

Before a week has gone by, more than half of the initially present radon atoms will no longer exist: more than half of them will have disintegrated.

But if your house is built of materials that contain radium, thorium, uranium, or certain other heavy elements, or if the underlying earth contains such materials, radon is being produced all the time and is entering the air in your house.

ORIGIN OF RADON

The radon nuclei that exists today in the air and in the ground were not always here. They were not here when the earth was formed.

They have been *created* here—created relatively recently. They are continually being created from heavier nuclei, especially uranium and thorium. The radon nuclei are produced indirectly: uranium and thorium atoms disintegrate and some of their disintegration products disintegrate in turn and produce radon nuclei. Specifically:

Uranium produces a chain of disintegrations. One product is the radium-226 nucleus which in turn disintegrates into ^{222}Rn.

Thorium produces a chain of disintegrations. One product is the radium-224 nucleus which in turn disintegrates into ^{220}Rn.

(Less important is actinium, which produces radium-223 and ^{219}Rn.)

The commonest types of radon nuclei are ^{222}Rn and ^{220}Rn.

HALF-LIVES OF THE COMMONEST RADON NUCLEI

The half-life of ^{222}Rn is 4 days. If you have a large quantity of the radon at a given time, about half of it will be gone (will no longer exist) after 4 days.

The half-life of ^{220}Rn is 1 minute.

These are short half-lives! Things happen fast; hence, the threat to health of persons exposed to radon. (If the half-lives were a million years, say, as is true of certain other kinds of radioactive nuclei, disintegrations would be so infrequent as to pose only a very small threat.)

WHAT IS THE RADON DISINTEGRATION PROCESS?

What, exactly, happens when a radon nucleus disintegrates? The radon nucleus itself ceases to exist and (within a trillionth of a second) these three new particles spring into being:

One slightly lighter nucleus (polonium nucleus).

One much lighter nucleus (helium nucleus, also called alpha particle).

One bit of electromagnetic energy (one photon of gamma radiation).

The lion's share of the energy released in the disintegration process is carried by the helium nucleus (i.e., alpha particle). At the instant of its creation it has about 6 million electron volts (Mev) of energy. This energy has the form of kinetic energy: the particle is traveling at very high speed.

A much smaller share is carried by the photon: about 1 Mev. The photon travels, of course, at the speed of light: 3×10^8 m/sec. Only a trivial amount of kinetic energy is carried by the (heavy!) polonium nucleus.

PHYSICAL DAMAGE

Tremendously disrupting effects are produced by the **helium** nucleus—in the matter that the nucleus travels through; more exactly, they are produced in the (solid or liquid) matter that lies within about 0.001 inch of the path taken by the nucleus. Why are the disrupting effects Large? Because:

1. The nucleus has an electric charge: a double charge (written ++). (Why does it have an electric charge? Because the nucleus travels "stripped," i.e., without its pair of electrons; accordingly the ++ charge of the nucleus is not neutralized.)

2. The nucleus is traveling at extremely high speed. A charged particle that is traveling at such speed does not swerve appreciably when it approaches a charged particle (positively charged nucleus or negatively charged electron); it may come extremely close to such particle and thus give it a large "jolt." Traveling in human tissue, for example, the fast, charged particle may knock some electrons out of some of the molecules, thus changing their chemical nature. Normal molecules (in living cells, for example) may be converted into abnormal molecules.

3. The nucleus travels a large distance (say, 1/10 inch), producing disruptions all along the way—about one million disruptions, for example.

The **photon** produces a smaller, but still important, amount of disruption. The amount is smaller because the photon has no electric charge and accordingly loses energy only slowly, i.e., in well-separated encounters. Only a slight amount of damage is done in any 1/10-inch segment of path. In other words, the physical effects produced by the photon are spread out and have only minor significance at any one spot.

The immediate damage done by the **polonium nucleus** is negligible—because this nucleus, being very heavy, has little speed, little kinetic energy. (Of course, much damage is done by the polonium nucleus later, i.e., when it disintergrates.)

RADON DAUGHTERS

By "radon daughters" (or radon decay products) one means a succession of nuclei formed by a succession of disintegrations. Typically there is a chain, or series, of disintegrations, with about four members ot the series. Thus the set might more properly be called radon's daughters, granddaughters, great-granddaughters, and great-great-granddaughters. Because there are several types of radon, there are many kinds of daughters—about a dozen in all. All are massive (only slightly lighter than radon itself) and all disintegrate energetically. Three disintegrate especially energetically. All of the radon daughters have atomic numbers of 83, 84, or thereabouts.

Are the chains, or series, extremely long? No. Each stops when the resulting heavy nucleus is a stable form of lead. (Lead is the 82nd element, and the lead nucleus ^{206}Pb is stable.)

What are the half-lives of the main radon daughters? About 10 or 100 minutes, typically. Some of the half-lives are 10 or 100 times shorter, and some are much longer.

The four most potentially harmful radon daughters are ^{214}Bi, ^{214}Pb, ^{214}Po, and ^{218}Po.

UNIT AMOUNT OF RADIOACTIVITY

The *curie* (abbreviated Ci) is the usual unit of measurement of the radioactivity of a large quantity of radon, radon daughters, or other radioactive material. It is defined as that quantity of nuclei of the specified material—radon, for example—that provides 3.7×10^{10} disintegrations per second.

Notice that the type, or violence, of the disintegrations is not taken into account—as far as this particular unit is concerned. Accordingly the unit is *not* a unit of energy release, or damage to material, or harm to living matter. Thus the significance, or usefulness, of the unit is limited.

But the unit has this in its favor: it can be cleanly defined, and it clears the way for a simple and accurate method of measurement. Counting of disintegrations is easily accomplished with a variety of low-cost instruments, e.g., Geiger counters, scintillation counters.

Usually, amounts of radioactivity are specified in terms of pico-curies (pCi).

One $pCi = 10^{-12}Ci$. It corresponds to about 2 disintegrations per minute.

HOW DO RADON AND RADON DAUGHTERS
ENTER THE INDOOR AIR?

Radon and radon daughters enter mainly from the earth (soil, rocks, groundwater, etc.) that is close beneath the house. The process starts with uranium and thorium in the ground. These materials produce, over the course of millions of years, radium. The radium produces radon. Although the uranium and thorium (in granite, for example) are relatively immobile, the radon can move easily because it is a gas; it dissolves in groundwater and drifts along with it. Eventually the radon may reach the surface of the earth -- surface of the crawlspace of a building, for example. Thus much radon may get into the building *from below*.

Does concrete contain radon? Usually not. Only in regions where radioactive materials are mined and the mine debris may be used in the making of concrete does one have to worry that the concrete itself may be a source of radon.

A little radon enters a house along with the infiltrating ambient air. This radon may come from many miles away. (But not much comes from air that has been at high altitude, because air that is at high altitude usually stays at high altitude for many months and, by that time, most of the included radon atoms will have disintegrated.) Some radon is "born" inside the human body. A typical person contains 3×10^{-11} gram of radium, which disintegrates (with very long half-life) into many radioactive products, including radon. Some radium atoms that are in indoor air disintegrate there, producing "born indoors" radon daughters.

CAN THE INFLUX OF RADON FROM THE EARTH
BENEATH A BUILDING BE STOPPED?

Yes. It can be stopped by installing an airtight barrier (an ordinary vapor barrier, say) at the surface of the crawl space earth. Or by providing a concrete basement floor. If the concrete floor of a basement contains cracks, it is important to seal all of these. Sealing merely 80% does little good, because the radon then enters through the remaining cracks. An important point is, the radon has a half-life of only a few days; if its trip from earth to indoor air is slowed sufficiently that the trip takes several weeks, nearly all of the radon will have disintegrated before it reaches the indoor air. That is, merely *slowing* the radon's travel may suffice.

Why do not the disintegration products of radon carry on and reach the indoor air? The most important disintegration products are elements that are normally solid, hence not highly mobile. They are not gases, and in particular they are not *noble* gases; thus they tend to stay put.

Of course, the provision of a concrete floor will not help much if the concrete itself contains much uranium and is itself producing radon.

Another way of preventing radon in the earth from diffusing upward into the basement is to use a very small exhaust fan to collect air from the bed of coarse gravel beneath the basement floor and discharge this air to outdoors. Thus any upward flowing radon will be intercepted and vented before it can enter the house proper.

Of course, an entirely different approach is to get rid of the radon gas *after* it enters the house— by using an air-to-air heat-exchanger. If an exchanger is needed in any event to dispose of excess humidity, formaldehyde, etc., using it to dispose of radon also will not cost anything extra!

For further information, see the EPA booklet "Radon Reduction Techniques for Detached Houses: Technical Guidance," EPA/625/5-86/019.

HOW DOES INDOOR RADON GET INTO THE HUMAN BODY?

Most radon enters the human body by inhalation: it enters when we breathe. It enters the windpipe, then the bronchi, then the microscopic pockets (alveoli) which have walls only a few molecules thick (to allow oxygen to pass through into the bloodstream and allow CO_2 to pass in the opposite direction).

Because radon is soluble in water, it may remain in the human body, and the resulting heavy radioactive atoms may lodge firmly within the body, doing considerable harm as they in turn disintegrate.

Radon atoms—in room air—tend to adhere to dust particles, and when these particles are inhaled and in turn adhere to the walls of the bronchi, trouble looms. The radon daughter atoms will remain in the bronchi for a relatively long time—a time long enough for the atoms to disintegrate and do harm. Some radon daughter atoms do not adhere to dust particles, and it is believed that these atoms, if inhaled, may be outstandingly harmful.

Small amounts of radon daughter atoms may enter the body via ingestion. Some of the food we eat contains traces of uranium, radium, radon, and radon daughters, and these may become incorporated in the body.

RADON HARM

It has been estimated (by C. D. Hollowell of Lawrence Berkeley Laboratory, per a recent article by Stephen Budiansky in *Environmental Science and Technology*) that indoor exposure to radon and radon daughters may be producing 1000 to 20,000 cases of death-from-lung-cancer each year in the United States.

It is now known (see Shapiro, 1981, p. 172) that the harmfulness of radon daughters (lodged in the bronchus of the lung) is 5 to 500 times the harmfulness of radon itself. The exact factor depends on just which part of the bronchus is under consideration and on the extent to which the bronchus is able to get rid of such radioactive atoms. There are several lung-cleaning mechanisms, for persons who do not smoke. For smokers, clearance is very slow—fatally slow in some instances. (Clearance is slow enough so that it is not of much help with respect to particles that disintegrate within a few days. This applies to smokers and non-smokers).

Clear symptoms of harm (from deposition of radon daughters in the lung) may be absent for many years. Harm may show up, often, 10 to 40 years later.

CONCENTRATIONS OF RADON IN OUTDOOR AIR AT GROUND LEVEL

Location	Concentrations of radon at ground-level locations	
	pCi/liter	pCi/m^3
Over large continents	0.1	100
Over coastal areas	0.01	10
Over oceans and arctic regions	0.001	1

These values are reported by Shapiro (1981). Note: the values given are for ^{222}Rn only. If ^{220}Rn were included, the values would be slightly higher. The values do not take radon daughters into account.

The global rate at which ^{222}Rn is emitted from land areas into the atmosphere is 50 Ci/sec. This corresponds to a rate of 0.4 pCi per second per square meter of land area.

The total amount of ^{222}Rn in the atmosphere at any given moment is 25,000,000 Ci.

CONCENTRATIONS OF RADON AND RADON DAUGHTERS IN HOUSES

Shapiro (1981) reports radon concentrations of:

0.01 to 0.2 pCi/liter in a brick apartment house in Boston, with a fresh-air input rate of 5 to 9 house-volumes per hour.

26 pCi/liter in an unventilated bedroom (in Chicago) over an unpaved crawl-space.

Representative value for the average concentration of ^{222}Rn in indoor air: 1 pCi/liter, according to Shapiro (1981, p. 364).

LIMIT ON PERMISSIBLE CONCENTRATION IN HOUSES

Radon concentrations are expressed in terms of *working level*. This unit may be defined as follows: suppose that there is, in each liter of air in a house, at noon today, enough of the important (short-lived) radon daughter atoms to produce, cumulatively and ultimately, enough alpha particles to deliver 130,000 Mev of energy. Then the concentration of radon daughters (in this house at noon today) is said to be one working level (WL).

The main recommendation is that, in houses in the United States, the concentration of radon daughters should not exceed 0.01 or 0.02 WL—and that at the very worst it should not exceed 0.05 WL. (Obviously, such a recommendation is not simple and businesslike. Presumably any *firm standard* announced will be fully businesslike.) Recommendations such as are stated above may be found in the US Federal Register *44* 38664 1979 in a document prepared by the U.S.

Environmental Protection Agency, and may be found also in a report issued by the U.S. Surgeon General. The recommendations were drawn up in connection with problems arising in certain parts of Colorado and Florida, where dangerously high levels of indoor radioactivity had been found. Somewhat similar limits have been proposes by the Canadian government.

Persons routinely working 170 hours a month at jobs involving exposure to radon and radon daughters are permitted to experience higher concentrations during their working hours: about 0.3 WL (time-averaged). Thus each year they may receive, while at work, up to 12 x 0.3 WL = about 4 Working Level Months. (A Working Level Month is the exposure, or dose, received by a person exposed for 170 hours to 1 WL.) Note that the level pertinent to working hours—0.3 WL—is 15 times the above-mentioned 0.02 WL level pertinent to the general public.

If the limit 0.02 WL is to be respected, how does the rate of fresh-air infiltration affect the limit on concentration of radon? Three cases must be considered:

Case 1. In a house that has a typical amount of infiltration, a general assumption is made to the effect that about half of the radon daughter atoms play no part: they are not in the house (they escaped, or were never formed within the house in the first place) or, if they are in the house, they plate out onto (become permanently attached to) the walls, ceiling, etc.; thus, they have no chance of entering the lungs of any occupant of the house.

The other half of the radon daughter atoms remain in room air—free or attached to very tiny particles—and may be inhaled and may lodge in the bronchi or lungs. The fraction of the atoms in question that remain in the room air, free or attached to particles (more exactly, the fraction of the energy deposition capability associated with the alpha particles from these atoms), is called the *equilibrium factor*. In the present case (house with typical amount of infiltration) the equilibrium factor is 0.5 and the 0.02 WL limit corresponds to (makes permissible) a radon concentration of about 4 picocuries per liter.

Case 2. In a house that is very tightly built, an equilibrium factor of about 0.75 may be assumed. Thus, to keep within the 0.02 WL limit, one must restrict the radon concentration to about 3 pCi/liter.

Case 3. The house is ideally tightly built and none of the radon daughters plate out: all remain airborn and can be inhaled. Here the equilibrium factor is about 1.0. Then 0.02 WL corresponds to about 2 pCi/liter.

These conclusions may be paraphrased thus: Concentrations should be kept below 4, 3, and 2 pCi/liter for houses that are typically tight, very tight, and ideally tight and non-plating.

Note: A person spending a full year in a house in which the concentration of ^{222}Rn is 1 pCi/liter will receive a whole-lung dose of 600 mrem and a basal-cells-of-the-bronchial-epithelium dose of 3200 mrem, "… assuming an equilibrium factor of 0.5," according to Shapiro. (The unit *mrem*, or milli-roentgen-equivalent-man, is usually used when the entire human body is exposed to a given amount of radiation. The unit is such that about 500,000 mrem has a 50-50 chance of killing a person. A dose of 5,000 mrem per year has often been considered acceptable for radiation workers. A dose of 600 mrem just to the whole lung—not to the entire body—is thus very small compared to the dose considered acceptable for radiation workers.)

Some Unanswered Questions Concerning Permissible Amount

Should there be just one published value of *permissible amount*, or should there be different values for different parts of the country, different kinds of terrain, different climates (very cold; not cold), different kinds of houses, different ages of house occupants?

Is the published *permissible amount* in line with other threats to health? Should it be applied even to those persons who habitually smoke, drink, overeat, drive recklessly, etc? Should it be applied to persons who are too poor to keep their houses warm in winter, too poor to buy air-to-air heat-exchangers? Should it be applied in an era when there is a real threat of a nuclear war?

Overall Harm to Persons in USA

It has been estimated (by C.D. Hollowell of Lawrence Berkeley Laboratory, per a recent article by Stephen Budiansky in *Environmental Science and Technology*) that indoor exposure to radon and radon daughters may be producing 1,000 to 20,000 cases of death from lung cancer each year in the United States.

HOME MONITORS OF RADON

Recently several types of home monitors of radon concentration have become commercially available. Some are simple to use and inexpensive. Others are more versatile and produce results more promptly—but are expensive and require the help of an expert.

The commonest simple, low-cost radon monitor is an activated charcoal cannister that is exposed to room air for a few days, then mailed to a qualified laboratory for evaluation. Cost: $10 to $25. In 1987 the Colorado Department of Health began installing 3,000 such cannisters in houses picked at random, in order to obtain a good idea of typical radon levels in Colorado houses.

Some commercial laboratories that supply and evaluate charcoal devices are:

Key Technology, Inc., 2503 Heilmandale Road, Jonestown PA 17038. Tel: (717) 867-5475.

Teledyne Isotopes, 50 Van Buren Avenue, Westwood NJ 07675. Tel: (201) 664-7070.

Air-Chek, P.O. Box 100, Penrose NC 28766. Tel: (800) 257-2366.

Another common kind is an alpha track detector, which contains a special plastic piece and a filter. Alpha particles leave permanent tracks in the plastic piece, and these can be counted by laboratory technicians employing microscopes. This detector also is inexpensive ($20 to $60) and can be sent by mail. An in-home exposure time of several weeks (sometimes several months) is recommended.

Commercial laboratories that supply and evaluate such devices include:

Terradex Corp, 460 North Wiget Lane, Walnut Creek CA 94598. Tel: (415) 938 2545

R. S. Landauer Jr. & Co., Division of Tech/Ops, 2 Science Road, Glenwood IL 60425.

In all, a great many companies supply and/or evaluate radon monitors. They are listed in the EPA pamphlet "Radon/Radon Progeny Measurement Proficiency Program," EPA-520/1-87-002, obtainable from regional EPA offices.

An especially versatile device (developed by Sun Nuclear Corporation, 415-C Pineda Court, Melbourne FL 32940) employs a solid-state sensor that responds to alpha particles in air—alpha particles from radon disintegration. Indicator lights of different color indicate different concentrations of radon. The device has the added capability of turning on an alarm or a fan whenever the radon concentration exceeds a given threshhold. Other capabilities include remote indication of radon concentration and automatic recording of concentration from hour to hour. Price: about $250.

At a cost of about $1,900 US, one can obtain a radon "working level" monitor that provides digital-type readings almost instantly. Called "Radon Sniffer" and intended for use by professionals, the device is obtainable from Thomson & Nielsen Electronics Ltd., 4019 Carling Avenue, Suite 202, Kanata, Ontario, Canada K2K 2A3. Weighing only one pound, the device is hand-held and operated off line or battery.

EPA PAMPHLETS

In 1986 and 1987 the U.S. Environmental Protection Agency (EPA) prepared and issued several pamphlets on radon hazards: sources of radon, how to prevent it from accumulating in the home, how to measure radon concentrations, etc. Some of the main pamphlets are:

A Citizen's Guide to Radon: What It Is and What to Do About It. Aug. 1986. Pamphlet OPA-86-004. 14 pp. Nine drawings.

Radon Reduction Methods: A Homeowner's Guide. Aug. 1986. Pamphlet OPA-86-005. 26 pp. Eleven drawings.

Interim Indoor Radon and Radon Decay Product Measurement Protocols. April 1986. Booklet EPA 520/1-86-04. 72 pp. No drawings. Written for officials, technicians, and monitor companies.

Radon Reduction Techniques for Detached Houses: Technical Guidance. June 1986. Booklet EPA/625/5-86/019. 60 pp. 14 drawings. Written for state radiological health officials, builders, and technically sophisticated homeowners.

Radon/Radon Progeny Measurement Proficiency Program. Jan. 1987. 18 pp. No drawings. Long list of companies qualified to evaluate seven kinds of radon monitors. Written for officials and monitor companies.

Interim Protocols for Screening and Followup Radon and Radon Decay Product Measurements. Feb. 1987. 28 pp. No drawings. Deals with monitoring strategies and with significance of results. Written for officials and monitor companies.

EPA ADDRESSES

The headquarters office of the US Environmental Protection Agency is in Washington, DC 20460. Most of its work is directed from the regional offices, which have the following addresses:

EPA Region 1, Room 2203, JFK Federal Building, Boston MA 02203. Tel: (617) 223-4845.
EPA Region 2, 26 Federal Plaza, New York NY 10278. Tel: (212) 264-2515.
EPA Region 3, 841 Chestnut Street, Philadelphia PA 19107. Tel: (215) 597-8320.
EPA Region 4, 345 Courtland Street N.E., Atlanta GA 30365. Tel: (404) 881-3776.
EPA Region 5, 230 S. Dearborn Street, Chicago IL 60604. Tel: (312) 353-2205.

EPA Region 6, 1201 Elm Street, Dallas TX 75270. Tel: (214) 767-2630.
EPA Region 7, 726 Minnesota Avenue, Kansas City KS 66101. Tel: (913) 236-2803.
EPA Region 8, Suite 1300, One Denver Place, 999 18th Street, Denver CO 80202. Tel: 9303) 283-1710.
EPA Region 9, 215 Fremont Street, San Francisco CA 94105. Tel: (415) 974-8076.
EPA Region 10, 1200 Sixth Avenue, Seattle WA 98101. (206) 442-7660.

An excellent source of technical information is: Center for Environmental Research Information, EPA, 26 West St. Clair Street, Cincinnati OH 45268.

RECOMMENDED TEST SEQUENCE

It is generally recommended that if the homeowner's house is located in a region where radon hazards have been reported, he should make a quick, rough test ("screening measurement") to find whether the radon level exceeds 1.0 WL or exceeds 200 pCi/liter.

If it does, the owner should consult with local health authorities, take immediate steps to reduce the radon level, and plan a follow-up test. If the level is ten-fold less, there is less urgency, but certainly a follow-up test should be made. If the level is a hundred-fold less, a cautious homeowner will arrange a long-term (many month) test. If the level is below 0.02 WL or 4 pCi/liter, a follow-up test is probably not needed. (For further details, see EPA pamphlet OPA-86-004.)

Usually the monitor should be placed in a room assumed to have the highest level of radon, for example, a ground-floor living room or bedroom that has no local forced ventilation. (A kitchen or bathroom that has an exhaust fan is not a good location.)

Chapter 12
Other Pollutants

Here a great many common pollutants of room air are discussed. They are much simpler than radon, and so the discussions can be brief. Most of the pollutants are generated within the house. These are discussed first.

POLLUTANTS GENERATED WITHIN THE HOUSE

These include:

Water vapor (H_2O) from cooking activity, showers, dish washers, clothes dryers, occupants' breathing, occupants' perspiration.

Carbon monoxide (CO) from gas stove, wood stove, fireplace.

Carbon dioxide (CO_2) from gas stove, wood stove, fireplace, occupants' breathing.

Formaldehyde (HCHO) from plywood, particleboard, adhesives, insulation, furniture padding. Other aldehydes.

Chemical sprays, e.g., for killing flying or crawling insects.

Particulates (respirable suspended particles) from general dust, smoke from gas stove or wood stove, smoke from cigarettes, etc. The diameters of pertinent particulates range from 0.001 to 100 um. Wood stoves produce some "polycyclic organic materials" (POMs) some of which may be carcinogenic.

Usually only negligible quantities of the following materials are generated within the rooms:

Nitrogen monoxide (NO).

Nitrogen dioxide (NO_2).

Sulfur dioxide (SO_2).

Ozone (O_3).

Asbestos.

Lead (Pb).

Water soluble nitrates (molecules containing the group NO_3).

Water soluble sulfates (molecules containing the group SO_4).

POLLUTANTS ENTERING FROM OUTDOORS

Country houses and city houses that have leaky roofs and are situated in regions having much rainfall may be plagued with excessive moisture. Country houses may be polluted by suspended organic matter (spores, e.g.) that enters from outside. Sprays used to improve garden crops, trees, etc. may pose problems. City houses may be polluted by a variety of chemicals produced by nearby automobile and truck traffic, factories, restaurants, etc. Such pollutants may enter a house via open doors or windows, or via air intakes for furnace, fireplace, etc., or via general infiltration. Sometimes the concentrations of pollutants in outdoor locations is greater than concentrations indoors. An air exchanger can actually *increase* the indoor concentrations of such materials.

WHAT FACTORS MAKE THE POLLUTANT CONCENTRATIONS HIGH?

Obviously, the concentrations will be high if the natural rate of infiltration is very low, because
• The house is protected from the wind—protected by nearby hills, buildings, woods.
• There are no chimneys. Or there are chimneys but they have been equipped with tight-fitting dampers.
• Vents intended to serve the kitchen and bathroom are kept shut.
• There are no blowers or equivalent for expelling stale air and bringing in fresh air.
• The rate of indoor generation of pollutants (or introduction of pollutants) is high.
• The general construction of the house (walls, roof, and basement) is very tight. This may be the case if

Much use is made of large, low-permeance, snugly installed plates of Thermax, Styrofoam, Thermoply, or the like in the external walls.

Much use is made of vapor barriers; no holes have been cut in them; edges are overlapped and sealed.

There are few external doors and windows, and such doors and windows have been caulked or weatherstripped.

Entrances are of vestibule (air-lock) type.

External doors and windows are seldom opened.

WHAT HARM DO THE POLLUTANTS DO?
WHAT CONCENTRATIONS ARE HARMFUL?

In general, clear and accurate answers are not yet available. Information is fragmentary.
Bad smells are usually relatively harmless. Annoying, yes. But they utsually produce little demonstrable harm.

Humidity is roublesome if too high or too low. See Chap. 4.

N_2O, NO, NO_2 are gases that can harm lung tissue. Permissible indoor concentrations have not yet been finally established (0-145).

Formaldehyde vapor in concentrations exceeding $100ug/m^3$ causes irritation to eyes and upper respiratory systems (F-700). In the Netherlands a limit of $120 ug/m^3$ has been proposed (F-700). Some proposed upper limits on indoor concentrations: California and Wisconsin, 200 ppb; Denmark and Netherlands, 100 to 120 ppb (0-145).

CO 50 ppm 8-hr. average is OSHA occupation standard. 30 ppm is 1-hr. National Ambient Air Quality Standards limit.

CO_2 500 ppm for 8-hrs exposure indicated by ASHRAE (F-700).

O_3 0.08 ppm (F-700).

A research group at the University of California has tried out various methods of measuring the concentrations of pollutants in typical houses. Details are given in Ref. 0-145.

STRATEGIES FOR REDUCING THE CONCENTRATIONS

Among the available strategies are:

"Forbid" the concentration. Prohibit smoking. Prohibit cooking cabbage. Prohibit use of sprays. Prohibit long showers.

Remove the source of pollution. Transfer the source to an outdoor shed or city dump.

Block off the polluting object. For example, cover the earth floor of a crawlspace with a plastic sheet impervious to radon and moisture.

Keep the house under slight positive pressure, to reduce the tendency for radon to seep upward from the ground into the house.

Provide local ventilation where there is an especially bothersome source.

Provide general ventilation, as by means of an air-to-air heat-exchanger.

Employ electrostatic precipitators of air filters (of fibrous or charcoal type.)

Open windows and doors.

Of course, persons building and furnishing houses should try to pick a site where little radon is present in the earth, use building materials that are free of pollutants, and select furnishings that are non-polluting.

SOURCES OF INFORMATION

There was a major conference on indoor air pollution on October 13-16, 1981, at Amherst, Massachusetts. Organized by Harvard University public health experts and government experts, the conference was called "International Symposium on Indoor Air Pollution, Health and Energy Conservation." About 100 papers were presented on nearly all aspects of indoor pollution, including: the pollutants, their abundance, their sources, their harmfulness, monitoring methods, and air-to-air heat-exchangers.

A comprehensive report on indoor pollutants was published later in 1981 by the National Academy of Sciences, 2100 Constitution Avenue, Washington DC 20418. Prepared by the Academy's Committee on Indoor Pollutants, the report contains much material on radon and other pollutants. See Bibl. item N-25.

Chapter 13
Energy, Heat and Heat Flow

This is not a book on energy or heat. Nevertheless, some facts about these basic concepts, and about enthalpy, are worth including. Enthalpy is unfamiliar to many people, yet it is easy to understand; it plays a dominant role in discussions of exchangers that transfer both heat and moisture.

ENERGY

The very foundation of physics and engineering is energy. It is all around us. No action can be initiated wtihout it. It is the common currency of action and change. Equations and formulas involving energy can be simple because of this simplifying fact, or law: the overall amount of energy in any system (any closed system) is constant. It cannot be increased. Cannot be decreased. It remains the same forever. This gives physicists a big head start at writing formulas involving energy.

What is energy, exactly? It is the capability to do something; for example, to lift a heavy weight, accelerate an automobile, produce electricity, warm some air, operate a blower, or evaporate some water. A kind of ultimate "acid test" for energy is: can it impart heat to some extremely cold material? Only energy fills this bill. (Speed, momentum, force, etc., cannot impart heat to a cold material. Only energy can.)

There are many kinds of energy. From time to time, additional kinds have been discovered, for example, nuclear energy or mass energy. Some of the commonest kinds are heat, energy of motion (kinetic energy), gravitational potential energy, chemical energy, electrical energy, and radiant energy (associated with visible radiation, ultraviolet, x-rays, gamma-rays, infrared and radio waves).

Units of Energy

The commonest units of energy are:

British thermal unit (Btu), defined as the amount of energy needed to raise the temperature of one pound of water one degree F. Originally applied just to heat, but later applied to all kinds of energy.

Joule (J), defined as one watt-second. Applicable to all kinds of energy. In most countries of the world it is the preferred unit.

1 Btu = 1055 J. 1 J = 9.478 x 10^{-4} Btu.

1 Btu = 2.931 x 10^{-4}kWh. 1 kWh = 3412 Btu.

Limitations on the Concept of Energy

The concept of energy has this Achilles' heel: to compute (or merely to define!) the total energy of a system—including *every* kind of energy it may contain—is virtually impossible.

Leaf through a half-dozen books on physics and see whether any of them ever discuss true total amount of energy. I predict that none of them do. Or ask any physics professor: "What is the total amount of energy in one pound of 70°F water in my kitchen?" I predict that you will get a lecture, but no number.

Seldom are persons interested in the *total* amount of energy in a system; they are usually interested in one kind of energy only—for example heat energy, or electrical energy. And, even with respect to one kind of energy, they are seldom interested in the *total amount*; they are usually interested in energy changes or energy increments; they want to know "How much energy does this process add, or take away? How much energy can be recovered?"

In calculating the energy of a system, an engineer may arrive at very different answers, depending on how many kinds of energy he chooses to include. If he is interested in heating a house deep in the woods of Vermont, he may include only (a) sensible heat, (b) the chemical energy in firewood, and (c) radiant energy from the sun.

Also, he may get very different answers depending on what assumptions he makes as to the surroundings, that is, assumptions as to what the energy is *relative to*. Does a small stone beneath his foot have zero potential energy? Does your answer change if he tells you that he is standing high up on a mountain?

From decade to decade new forms of energy are discovered. An engineer back in 1900, on inspecting a hunk of uranium, would have declared it to have almost no energy. Today, every engineer would give a very different answer. Thus our appraisals of the energy of a system may change as our understanding of the physical universe grows.

The consequence of these difficulties concerning energy is that engineers usually confine their attention to limited classes of energy and to increments within such classes. For example, they may deal just with heat, or, more exactly, additions and subtractions of heat. They may deal also with so-called latent heat, or internal energy, or enthalpy (defined in a later paragraph).

HEAT

This is one of the commonest forms of energy. It is the energy associated with the random motions of atoms and molecules. The more rapidly they move about and vibrate and rotate, the more heat they contain. Note that, because heat is a combination of myriad random motions, heat cannot be manipulated in a simple and concise way; thus it differs importantly from light, electricity, etc., which we can control and transform with great elegance. Always heat is a grand mixture of kinds and quantities of motion; it can be dealt with only in an overall, statistical way; in a sense it is a vulgar, intractable kind of energy.

The amount of heat in a system (more exactly, the amount above some arbitrary reference level) is given the symbol **Q**, for **quantity**.

Heat is called an **extensive** quantity: the amount of heat in a system depends directly on the size of the system. Double the size, and you double the amount of heat. The amount of heat in the oceans is enormous, even though they are only lukewarm in temperature at best! The amount of heat in a cup of boiling water is trifling, even though the temperature of the water may be extremely high. (Temperature is an **intensive**—not extensive—property.)

Infrared Radiation Is Not Heat

Electromagnetic radiation (light, infrared, radio waves, etc.) is not heat. Electromagnetic radiation can be manipulated in a concise way: it can be reflected, focused, polarized, etc. Heat cannot. Many authors who write about infrared radiation mistakenly call it a form of heat. It is not heat. No electromagnetic radiation is heat. Any kind of such radiation, when absorbed, can *produce* heat, i.e., can be converted to heat. In this respect, infrared radiation is no different from light, radio waves, etc.: they too, on being absorbed, are entirely converted to heat.

TEMPERATURE

Temperature is a measure of the violence of the random motions of atoms and molecules. It is an intensive parameter, not an extensive one. That is, it is not influenced by how much matter you have, but only by the violence of the random motions.

The commonest units of temperature are: degree Fahrenheit (F or °F) and degree Celsius (C or °C). 32°F and 212°F correspond to 0°C and 100°C respectively. To convert from Fahrenheit to Celsius, subtract 32 and multiply by 5/9.

The Rankine scale is like the Fahrenheit scale but starts at absolute zero. Thus the Fahrenheit values 0, 32, 70, 100, correspond to 459.67, 491.67, 529.67, and 559.67 Rankine. To convert to Rankine, add 459.67. The Kelvin scale is like the Celsius scale but starts at absolute zero. Thus 0, 20, and 100°C correspond to 273.15, 293.15, and 373.15 K.

ENTHALPY

Enthalpy is to heat as apple pie a-la-mode is to ordinary apple pie. It is a combination: an especially happy combination. It is the combination of *heat energy* and *"pressure-volume"* energy. Called H, it is expressed as:

$$H = U + pV$$

where U is the heat (also called—not very appropriately—internal energy), p is the pressure of the system, and V is the volume of the system.

One assumes that the system consists just of a single small chamber containing just gas—so that one value of pressure characterizes the entire system.

Enthalpy is a key, or the key, parameter in many calculations involving energy transfer, energy recovery, or energy saving—specifically those calculations that involve the combination of heat and pressure-volume energy. If a quantity of air is warmed up, the heat is increased. If a small amount of water evaporates into this air, the pressure-volume energy is increased. If both processes occur at once, both kinds of energy are increased, which may be summarized by saying that the enthalpy increases. And it is this overall quantity—enthalpy—that really counts. Why? When two kinds of energy change occur, the law of conservation of energy does not apply to either alone: it applies only to the combination, i.e., the enthalpy. The "bottom line" is enthalpy. What the designer is trying to conserve, ordinarily, is enthalpy.

Warning: This is not always the goal. If, in winter, a house contains much air that is warm, stale, and too humid, the occupant's goal, in using a heat-exchanger, is to bring in fresh air and expel (not save!) moisture. He desires to expel moisture even if this entails a loss of enthalpy.

HEAT FLOW

The total amount of heat that has flowed from one body to another in a given time interval is called Q, and the amount that flows each second is called q. *Btu* is a common unit of amount of heat.

Heat may flow by any and all of these three mechanisms: (1) conduction, in which the matter stays roughly fixed but the energy (kinetic energy of atoms and molecules) moves along, (2) convection, involving gross travel of material, e.g., water or air, and (3) radiation.

Everything is emitting electromagnetic radiation at all times (everything that is hotter than absolute zero) and in all directions. Likewise, everything is receiving and absorbing such radiation at all times. Emission tends to make an object cooler, and absorption tends to make it hotter. What counts, usually, is the difference between amount emitted and amount absorbed. Often this difference is very small, in which case heat flow by radiation can be disregarded.

AIR FLOW

In a house served by an air-to-air heat exchanger, either of two measures of airflow rate may be used:

The simple rate: number of cubic feet of air flowing per minute. The unit is called **cfm**, cubic feet per minute.

The rate relative to the volume of the house, with the unit of time chosen to be one hour. Thus the overall unit is "house volumes per hour," or V_H, where V stands for volume and H stands for house.

Given the plans of a house, anyone can easily compute the volume of air in it. For instance, a typical 1,000 ft^2 house has a volume of about 8,000 ft^3:

$$V_H = 8,000 \text{ ft}^3$$

However, a question may arise as to whether to include the volume of air in the basement, crawl space, and attic. Are these to be considered regular parts of the house? Usually not—usually these regions are not occupied by people and not supplied with fresh air.

Chapter 14

Air-to-Air Heat Exchangers
of Fixed Type: Design Principles

In an air-to-air heat-exchanger of typical design there are two streams of air, separated by a set of thin sheets of metal or plastic through which heat can flow easily but no air can flow, and no water, whether in liquid or gaseous form, can flow. Each stream is driven by an electrically powered blower (or fan).

The intervening thin sheets may be flat, may be curved to form tubes, may be accordian folded, or may have other shapes. They may be called sheets, plates, membranes, septums, tubes, pipes, or ducts. The set or assemblage of such devices is called the exchanger proper, or core.

PRINCIPLE OF OPERATION

Because a stream of warm outgoing air "bathes" one side of each sheet and cold incoming air bathes the other side, one side is hotter than the other and accordingly heat flows through the sheet. By the time the outgoing air reaches the outdoors it has given up so much heat that it is nearly as cold as the outdoor air; correspondingly the incoming air, as it enters the room, has become nearly as warm as the indoor air. Overall, about 60 to 80% of the heat that would have been lost is recovered.

The blower in a given airstream may be situated upstream or downstream from the heat-transfer sheets. That is, it may be pushing or pulling air through the exchanger proper.

Filters may be provided in either or both of the airstreams. Usually each filter is located upstream from the exchanger proper; thus, it prevents dust from entering the exchanger proper and perhaps lodging there and restricting the slender passages and slightly reducing the rate of heat-flow through the thin sheets. The filters may have to be cleaned periodically.

The outdoor discharge location of the outgoing air is kept well separated from the outdoor air-intake location. Accordingly no appreciable amount of discharged air is reintroduced to the house.

The air to be discharged from the house may be drawn from one room (e.g., kitchen, bathroom, or other room where pollutant concentration may be especially high), or from several rooms. Likewise, the incoming fresh air may be delivered to one room (e.g., living room or other room where the house occupants spend much time) or to several rooms.

EXCHANGER PROPER

Many air-to-air heat-exchangers employ flat sheets. Some employ tubes or heat pipes. A typical sheet-type exchanger includes a large number of sheets arranged in a stack, with airspaces between sheets. Incoming air flows in Spaces 1, 3, 5, etc., and outgoing air flows in Spaces 2, 4, 6 etc. Thus the total area of heat-exchange surface may be very large while the length and breadth of the assembly are small.

A tube-type exchanger may include many tubes running parallel to one another, with spaces between. Outgoing air (say) flows in the tubes and the incoming air flows (in antiparallel direction or cross direction) in the spaces between them. Again a large area of heat-transfer is provided in a compact region. To save space and to improve heat-transfer, the designer usually chooses very small spacings and very small diameters.

FLOW-DIRECTION RELATIONSHIP

An interesting topic is the choice of relationship of the directions of the two airstreams. There are three distinct choices, each with its own advantages and disadvantages. Concurrent-flow streams have the same direction. Crossflow streams are at right angles to one another. Counterflow streams have opposite directions.

Counterflow exchangers can have very high efficiencies even when of modest overall dimensions—and, in principle, can have near-100% efficiency if the heat-exchanger area is extremely large. Cross-flow exchangers also can have very high efficiency, but this is attainable only if the heat-exchanger area is somewhat larger than that of a counterflow exchanger of equal efficiency. Concurrent flow exchangers have very low efficiency (well below 50%, usually) and are not discussed in this book.

To keep the two flowrates equal is often difficult. If there is slight deformation of the walls in one airstream but not the other, or if the flow-paths in one stream are more circuitous than those in the other airstream (in the header, or manifold, regions, say), or if one circuit has greater accumulation of dust or frost than the other has, the two flowrates may differ significantly. Differences in resistance along the two sets of ducts (serving the two airstreams) likewise may produce imbalance of flow.

BLOWERS, FANS AND MANIFOLDS

Blowers are preferred when the pressure head is large. Fans, sometimes called axial blowers, are preferred when the pressure head is small. Most air-to-air heat-exchangers employ blowers. Blowers are of centrifugal (squirrel-cage) type. The vanes that drive the air may be radial or may have forward (positive) or backward (negative) slant, positive slant being preferred if the pressure head is relatively small.

Specially shaped manifolds, or headers, are employed to introduce the airstreams to the pertinent passages within the exchanger proper and to receive the emerging air. The point is, of course, that the two streams must be kept separate at all times. If they become mixed, much of the air heading toward outdoors may soon find itself en route back to the rooms. Designing the manifolds is sometimes difficult (and making clear drawings of them is also difficult). If many airstream-direction changes are caused by the manifolds, the resistance to airflow is increased and higher power blowers may be required. Later chapters show the designs of many kinds of manifolds.

INSULATION AND ORIENTATION

Most heat-exchanger outer surfaces, or housings, are insulated—to minimize flow of heat to or from the general surroundings. Of course, such insulation is of small importance if the exchanger is very compact, i.e., has a small external surface area despite having a large total heat-transfer area. Ordinarily, however, the use of insulation is cost-effective. Insulation applied to the exchanger housing may be applied to the inner or outer face of the housing. Usually the inner face is preferred. Ducts are usually insulated externally. The commonest insulating material used is fiberglass.

Most exchangers can have a variety of orientations, subject only to the arrangement of drains for any liquid water that is produced. As far as airflow and heat-exchange are concerned, the airflow directions in the exchange proper may be east and west, north and south, up and down, or at any angle from such direction. Usually an exchanger is mounted slightly tilted, to assist drainage.

OPERATING PROCEDURE

The simplest procedure is to let the exchanger run continuously throughout the midwinter period—period when windows are kept closed. The cost of the electrical power for the blowers is small and the amount of heat lost (because the exchanger has an efficiency of less than 100%) may be acceptable.

Next simplest is to have the house occupants control the exchanger manually: turn it on when they deem appropriate and turn it off when they deem appropriate. Their actions are governed by their *sensations* as to whether moisture, smells, etc., are excessive and on *what they have heard or read* as to the threats posed by formaldehyde, radon, etc. But if the occupants are careless or forgetful the overall performance may be poor.

Automatic controls can be used, and, in principle, can regulate pollutant concentrations more reliably and more accurately. Sensors that respond to different levels of humidity already exist and are relatively simple. But to provide a set of sensors that respond to many kinds of pollutant (smells, formaldehyde, radon, humidity, etc.) would be very expensive. Perhaps inexpensive sets will be developed in the next few years.

For further details see Chapter 18.

TEMPERATURE DISTRIBUTION

In each airstream of a fixed-type exchanger there is a temperature distribution along the exchanger, i.e., along the air in any given slender passage. The distribution depends on many design parameters and also on the flowrates of the two airstreams.

If the two rates are equal and are extremely low, and if no condensation occurs, the temperature of the incoming air at successive locations along the exchanger (starting, say, from the cold end, here assumed to be the left end) is successively higher and the temperature of this air as it enters the room is almost as high as room temperature. The temperature of the outgoing air has a nearly identical distribution (again I assume that distance is measured from the cold end—left end). In other words, at any given location along the exchanger, the outgoing air has slightly higher—but *only* slightly higher—temperature than the incoming air (at this location).

The two distribution curves (see below) are nearly straight and they have (at any one location along the exchanger) identical slope, as must be the case inasmuch as the heat that is lost by one airstream is gained by the other. Obviously, the efficiency of sensible heat recovery, in the case under discussion, is very high. In drawing the graph I have assumed that the indoor and outdoor temperatures are 70°F and 30°F, the exchanger is 20 in. long, and the heat-exchanger efficiency is about 90%.

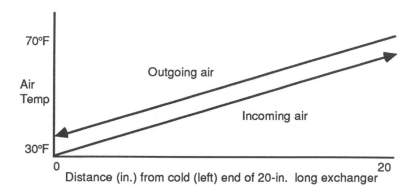

If the two rates of airflow are extremely high, the two distribution curves are again approximately straight lines and the slopes are identical, but the two curves are far apart: the incoming air never gets very warm and the outgoing air never gets very cold. The efficiency of sensible heat recovery is low—about 25% in the case depicted below.

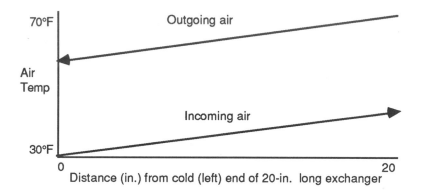

In practice the rates of airflow are chosen so as to provide a good compromise between the desire for high efficiency and the desire for a rapid rate of fresh air input. Achieving a good compromise is facilitated if the blowers are of variable-speed type, i.e., if the flowrates can be altered to accommodate varying circumstances.

WATER DRIP

Water is produced—by condensation from high-humidity air—when the outgoing stale air is cooled sufficiently drastically, that is, cooled more than enough to raise the relative humidity to 100%. When cooling proceeds beyond this extent, invisible gaseous H_2O molecules clump together to form visible droplets and form a fog; and soon the droplets join together to form drops large enough to settle rapidly onto the very same (very cold) walls that produced the cooling.

In the left graph below, the curves show the changes in condition of the outgoing air and incoming air when the cooling is slight. The relative humidity of the outgoing air increases but never reaches 100%; no condensation occurs. The curves of the graph on the right show what happens when the cooling is far more drastic: the outgoing air is cooled so drastically that moisture in the outoing air condenses and forms water, and eventually this water will drip and flow to a drain.

Notice that part of the upper curve is straight and horizontal; no condensation occurs here. But the left portion of this curve curves steeply downward—following the so-called saturation curve; here the process involves much condensation, much dripping of water.

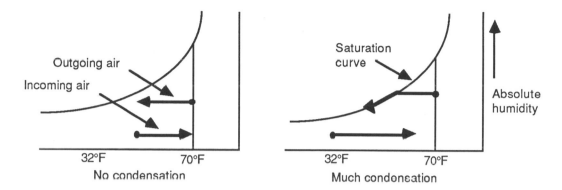

The beneficial effect of the condensation process is that it represents conversion of latent heat into sensible heat. The incoming air picks up more heat than would have been possible if no gaseous water had been converted to liquid water. Whenever a graph of change of condition of outgoing air has a sloping segment that coincides with the saturation curve, the exchange is recovering some heat that was latent but now has become sensible. Thus the exchanger is performing especially well: its efficiency of heat recovery is especially high.

WHEN IS ICE FORMED?

Ice—rather than water—is produced when the outgoing air is cooled so drastically that (1) it becomes saturated and begins to release aggregates of H_2O molecules, and (2) it is so cold that these aggregates at once form ice. When the outgoing air has traveled along through the exchanger and cooled down to 35 or 40°F, the condensate consists of liquid water, but when cooling continues down to temperatures well below 32°F, the condensate has the form of frost, or ice, that coats the walls of the (very cold) surfaces that produce the cooling. (These surfaces themselves are cooled, of course, by the extremely cold incoming air. As the incoming air is warmed, its relative humidity decreases; thus there is no tendency for any condensation of any kind to occur in the passages carrying incoming air.)

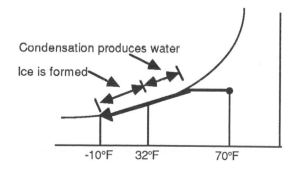

Notice that under no circumstances does an exchanger of this type recover any of the water that was in the outgoing airstream. The various surfaces of sheet metal or plastic are impervious to water; no water molecules can shift from one airstream to the other. (Exception: if an exchanger employs sheets of porous paper or other porous material, some transfer of water can occur.)

MEASURES OF PERFORMANCE

Rate of airflow, in cubic feet per minute (cfm), is of prime importance. An airflow of 50 cfm may be enough for a single room, but 100 to 300 cfm may be needed for a house as a whole. A 1500 ft^2 house with 8 ft ceiling height has a volume of about 12,000 ft^3; to bring in half this much air per hour (to provide what is called a half an air change per hour, 1/2 ACH) requires 6000/60 or 100 cfm. Of course faster fresh-air input may be needed if the house is very tightly built and contains major sources of pollution. (See the following section concerning standards established for ventilation rates.)

Efficiency of heat recovery is important also: important in minimizing the amount of auxiliary heat needed, and so minimizing the heating bill. Efficiency may be defined by this example: Suppose that the outgoing warm stale air is carrying 10,000 Btu of heat to the outdoors each hour, and suppose that the rates of flow of outgoing stale air and incoming fresh air are equal. Then if, each hour, 7,500 Btu of heat is transferred from the outgoing air to the incoming air, the efficiency of heat-transfer is 7,500/10,000 or 75%. (The industry usually calls this quantity "sensible recovery efficiency.") Some manufacturers prefer to state, for their exchangers, its "effectiveness"; the effectiveness figure includes heat produced by the blower motors, and so is higher than the efficiency figure—and less meaningful.

Power consumption is important, since the annual cost of electrical power to operate an exchange may be in the range $40 to $80, depending on the properties of the exchanger and the local cost of electricity.

Quietness of operation is also important, and the same is true of ease of control, ease of maintenance, reliability, durability, etc. A variety of controls are available, and it is important that they be chosen with due regard to the requirements of the house and the desires of the occupants.

Warning: Published figures on the airflows produced by exchangers, and on efficiencies, often require interpretation. The values depend greatly on the static pressure heads in the duct systems and on the choice of speed (low or high) of the blowers. Many other factors also (for example, ambient temperature and defrost cycles) influence the values. In earlier years many manufacturers published airflow and efficiency values that were decidely roseate. Even today, purchasers should retain some skepticism of published results that have not been verified by an independent laboratory. Some suppliers confuse effectiveness with efficiency—and so claim efficiency values that are too high.

PERFORMANCE STANDARDS

In recent years groups in Canada and the United States have established agencies to devise and publish standards: standard terminology, standard test methods, etc. These groups have made good progress at inducing the manufacturers to test their exchangers more fully and publish the results more carefully. Among the many groups concerned, the following have played the leading roles:

Canadian Standards Association (CSA), 178 Rexdale Boulevard, Rexdale, Ontario, Canada M9W 1K3.

CSA Standard C349 covers test equipment, methods, and calculations. Standard C444 Form A covers installation. Standard C22.2 covers fans and blowers.

American Society of Heating Ventilating and Air Conditioning Engineers (ASHRAE), 1791 Tullie Circle, Atlanta, GA 30329.

ASHRAE Standard 62-81, covering ventilation requirements (such as 100 cfm for kitchen, 50 cfm for each bathroom) has been adopted also by the Canadian Standards Assocation.

Heating, Refrigeration, and Air Conditioning Institute, 5468 Dundas St. West, Suite 226, Islington, Ontario, Canada M9B 6E3.

Home Ventilating Institute, 30 West University Drive, Arlington Heights, IL 60004.

The Home Ventilating Institute is a division of the Air Movement and Control Association.

Ontario Research Foundation, Sheridan Park, Missisauga, Ontario, Canada L5K 1B3.

The ORF has performed most of the formal testing of exchangers.

Chapter 15

Air-to-Air Heat Exchangers
of Rotary Type: Design Principles

Rotary type exchangers have played a major role in industrial plants, commercial buildings, etc., for more than 50 years. They can handle very large airflows, recover heat with high efficiency, recover sensible heat and latent heat, and, if this is desired, recover moisture also. They are compact and inexpensive.

But to designers of houses they are little-known. Until a few years ago most architects had not heard of rotary exchangers and in fact no rotary exchangers produced especially for use in houses were commercially available. Today, at least two manufacturers are mass-producing such devices.

Excellent discussions of large-size, industrial-use, rotary exchangers are included in the book *Energy Recovery Equipment and Systems: Air-to-Air* published by the Sheet Metal and Air Conditioning Contractors National Association (see Bibliography item S-162).

BASIC PRINCIPLES

A rotary exchanger, which is one class of reversing flow exchanger, employs a slowly rotating wheel, or rotor, that receives two adjacent airstreams of opposite direction. The rotor is massive and contains thousands of tiny passages parallel to the axis (and parallel to the airflows).

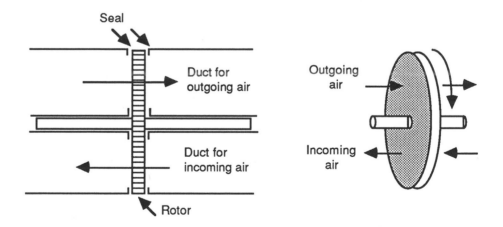

Each sector of the rotor passes across one airstream and then the other; it accepts heat from one and gives up heat to the other. The heat-exchange surface is so large that the efficiency of sensible-heat recovery is 70 to 90%, typically. Because 80 or 90% of the frontal area of the rotor is open, the pneumatic resistance is low and low-power blowers may be used.

In some kinds of rotary exchangers, desiccant has been incorporated in the heat-transfer material or surfaces, and accordingly water vapor may be absorbed from one airstream and delivered to the other. Thus latent heat, as well as sensible heat, may be recovered. The efficiency of overall recover (*enthalpy* recovery) may be 70 to 90%.

ROTOR

The rotor of a household-type rotary exchanger is 9 to 15 inches in diameter and 0.75 to 2.5 inches thick. Rotors for industrial exchangers may have diameters up to 14 feet and thicknesses up to 8 inches.

The rotor may be of aluminum, plastic (e.g., a Teflon-base plastic such as DuPont's Nomex), or other material.

The rotor includes thousands of slender passages for airflow. The passages are parallel to the rotor axis. Their cross-sectional shapes may be random, or triangular (honeycomb-like), or lenticular.

Passage diameters may be about 1/24 in. for small exchangers and two or three times as great for larger ones. Total surface area of the rotor is of the order of 100 ft ^{2}. About 80% of the total face-area of the rotor may be open, for small rotors, and about 90% for large ones.

The rotor may be strengthened by bands and spokes of steel. Sturdy and stable construction is needed so that the large temperature dfference across the wheel will not cause it to warp and bind against the sealing strips (discussed below).

The heat-transfer surfaces may be impregnated with a hygroscopic material, or desiccant, such as LiCl or silica gel. The desiccant must be non-deliquescent, i.e., must not dissolve in water and float away. The desiccant picks up water from the (high-humidity) outgoing air and dispenses the water to the incoming air.

The rotor is rotated slowly—5 to 25 times per minute—by a small motor situated adjacent to it and connected to it by a belt. In some installations the rotational speed is variable.

The typical linear speed of airflow in a passage in the rotor is of the order of 5 to 10 ft/sec.

DUCTS

The rotor is served by two parallel ducts, which may be semi-circular in cross section. The ducts carry the outgoing and incoming airstreams, which have opposite directions. Thus, as the rotor turns, a given passage may find itself carrying outgoing air for a few seconds, then incoming air for a few seconds, and so on. Each duct is served by its own centrifugal-type blower.

Plastic sealing strips are provided at each face of the rotor: they extend around the perimeter and also across the diameter that separates the two ducts. Such strips may consist of a compliant tube that presses gently against the rotor.

PURGE SECTOR

To reduce almost to zero the amount of air that can leak (at the rotor) from the outgoing airstream to the incoming airstream (thus posing the threat of contaminating the incoming air with toxic pollutants from the outgoing air), the designer sometimes provides a *purge sector*. This consists mainly of a baffle, shaped like a sector (piece of pie with 20-deg angle), mounted closely adjacent to the rotor at the location where the air passages from the outgoing airstream progress to the incoming airstream. Although essential in some exchangers used in chemical plants dealing with highly toxic gases, the purge sector is usually not needed in household devices. Some small contamination of incoming fresh air by outgoing stale air is of negligible consequence.

MOISTURE RECOVERY

Unlike exchangers of fixed-plate type, some rotary-type exchangers can recover water. This is true of exchangers whose rotor surfaces have been coated with a chemical (desiccant) that can readily absorb moisture from high-humidity air, and equally readily release such moisture to low-humidity air. Thanks to the desiccant coatings, water molecules from the outgoing airstream can actually be transferred to the incoming airstream, after the rotor has made approximately a half turn. Since the water molecules are—in both airstreams—in gaseous form, the heat recovery represented by this transfer is *latent* heat.

In the accompanying graph at the right both of the curves are sloping. That is, each implies a change of temperature and a change of moisture content. Neither curve has a horizontal segment. (Every curve applicable to an exchanger of fixed-metal-plate type has a horizontal segment—a segment implying change in temperature with no change in moisture content.)

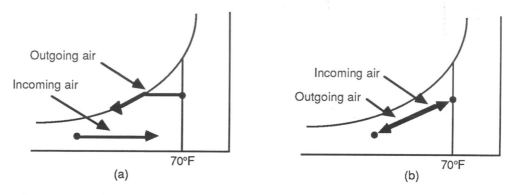

(a)   (b)

Is such recovery of latent heat (recovery in the form of gaseous H_2O) helpful? Only if the homeowner wishes to retain, or increase, the present relative humidity of room air. If the room air is already too humid, recovery of gaseous H_2O does more harm than good. It worsens the relative humidity and has no tendency to maintain room-air temperature. (These remarks deserve careful thought, because all too many persons tend to assume that, in winter, increased recovery of latent heat is good. It is good only if room air tends to be too dry.)

PRODUCTION OF WATER OR ICE

Because the curve pertinent to a desiccant-loaded rotary-type exchanger has a downward-to-the-left slope, the curve has less likelihood of reaching the saturation curve. Thus there is less likelihood of producing water or ice. Conditions must be considerably more extreme (than for exchangers of ordinary fixed-plate type) before water or ice is produced. Therefore, frost accumulation is less likely to occur. And when frost does occur, there is less of it. Why? Two easy answers are: (1) Because so much of the H_2O has gone back into the rooms, and (2) because the curve slopes down to the left and tend to "miss" the saturation curve. It is instructive to compare the two preceding graphs. The one at the left applies to a typical fixed-plate type of exchanger; notice that the upper curve follows the saturation curve for a considerable distance, implying formation of water and ice. In the graph at the right, the curves slope sufficiently steeply that the upper curve does not touch the saturation curve; no condensation occurs.

Chapter 16
Airflow Technology

The designer of an air-to-air heat-exchanger wants the device to transfer much heat but to occupy only a small space. Therefore he provides a large area of heat-transfer surface that is very compactly arranged. He provides dozens or hundreds of slender passages in which the incoming air and outgoing air flow, and he provides blowers to drive the two airflows.

The passages are usually so slender that, despite the fact that there are a great many of them in parallel, there is a significant pressure drop (back pressure) of about 0.2 to 0.8 in. of water.

Air filters, situated upstream from the set of passages, are used to intercept any dust particles that might clog the passages. The filters must be reasonably thin and open, otherwise they would greatly increase the pressure drop.

Ducts, usually about 3 to 6 in. diameter, may be needed to collect stale air from kitchen, bathrooms etc. and deliver it to the exchanger. The ducts add to the overall pressure drop, especially if they include many sharp bends.

In this chapter I discuss some general features of airflow in slender passages, ducts, etc., and I present data on blower performance. I start with a discussion of airflow in ducts, since this is a well-understood subject.

On the most important subject—air flow in very slender passages—I say very little. I have encountered very little information on this subject.

DISTRIBUTION OF AIR SPEED

When air is being driven steadily, in laminar flow, within a straight, circular-cross-section, smooth-walled duct, the speed is greatest along the axis (centerline) and is approximately zero at the wall. The speed varies "parabolically" with distance from the axis (see diagram of speed distribution to the right of figure).

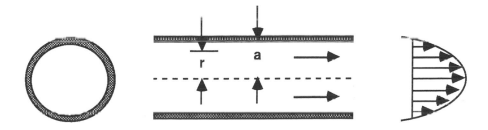

If the average speed of flow (over the cross section) is u_m and the duct radius is a, the speed u at some distance r from the axis is:

$$u = 2u_m (1 - r^2/a^2)$$

which, incidentally, implies that the speed of flow along the centerline of the duct is just twice the average speed.

Consider the quantity Q, which is the volume of air crossing a given cross section of the duct per second. Clearly $Q = \pi\, a^2 u_m$. How does Q depend on the pressure head? Consider some long central segment of the duct: a segment of length L. Suppose the air pressures at the two ends of the segment are p_1 and p_2. Then it has been found that

$$Q = \pi\, a^2\, u_m = \frac{\pi a^4\,(p_1 - p_2)}{8\mu\, L}$$

where μ is the viscosity of air. Notice that the volume flowrate is directly proportional to the pressure head $(p_1 - p_2)$.

Warning: These equations do not hold near the ends of the duct. Also they do not hold when the flow is turbulent.

DISTRIBUTION FOR TURBULENT-FLOW AIR

Here the velocity-vs-radial-position curve has a blunter peak, as suggested by the following sketch.

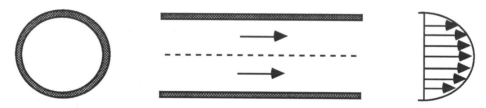

The shape of the curve is not parabolic, and indeed has no simple algebraic description. Also, the average speed of the air (average taken over the cross section of the duct) is about 0.8 times— not 0.5 times—the speed of air traveling along the duct axis. My understanding is that the average speed (and likewise the volume flowrate) is proportional to the *square root* of the pressure head.

PRESSURE DROP IN TURBULENT AIRFLOW IN A LONG, STRAIGHT DUCT OF CIRCULAR CROSS SECTION

When air at sea level and 70°F is traveling (with turbulent flow) at a volume flowrate of 100 cfm within a 3-in-diameter straight duct, there is a pressure drop along the duct (i.e., along the airstream within the duct). The pressure drop per 100-ft-length of duct is 3 in. of water (0.108 lb/in.^{2}). Incidentally, the linear velocity (averaged over the cross section of the duct) in this case is 34 ft/sec.

The following table shows the pressure drop (and linear airflow speed) for a variety of volume flowrates and duct diameters.

Example. What is the pressure drop in a 100-ft, 6-in.-diameter duct in which the volume rate of airflow is 512 ft^3/min.? Answer: 2 inches of water, per last entry in table.

The pressure drop is approximately proportional to the length. Thus the pressure drop along a duct of any given length L can be found by multiplying the pertinent number from the table by (L/100 ft).

Warning: The values listed above are for ducts that have extremely smooth walls. If the walls are rough, the pressure drops may be much greater.

Pressure drop (in. of water) in turbulent airflow in 100-ft-long, straight, circular-cross-section duct. Also linear speed of airflow (ft/min).

Volume flowrate (ft^3/min.)	8	16	32	64	128	256	512
	Duct diameter—1.5 in.						
Pressure drop	0.8	3	10				
(Linear speed)	(650)	(1300)	(2600)				
	Duct diameter—2 in.						
	0.2	0.6	2.3	9			
	(400)	(700)	(1400)	(3000)			
	Duct diameter—3 in.						
	0.025	0.1	0.3	1	4	13	
	(150)	(330)	(600)	(1200)	(2600)	(5000)	
	Duct diameter—4 in.						
			0.09	0.3	1	3.5	
			(400)	(750)	(1500)	(3000)	
	Duct diameter—5 in.						
				0.1	0.4	1.5	5
				(500)	(1000)	(1900)	(3800)
	Duct diameter—6 in.						
					0.15	0.6	2
					(700)	(1400)	(2800)

EFFECT OF A NINETY-DEGREE BEND IN DUCT

Suppose that a circular-cross-section duct includes a 90-degree change in direction, accomplished by a smooth, quarter-circular segment, the centerline of which has a radius of curvature that happens to be identical to the diameter of the duct. Experiments have shown that the added pressure drop (due to the 90-degree bend) is the same as that which would be produced by adding a straight section (of the same diameter) that has a length equal to 16 pipe diameters. (It is assumed here that the linear speed of flow is great enough so that the flow is turbulent.)

Sometimes 90-degree bends are accomplished by an elbow that has 2, 3, 4, or more straight segments, as suggested by the following sketches. Employing more segments (to make the bend a better approximation to a smooth quarter-circle) reduces the friction. Also, changing to an elbow of greater effective radius-of-curvature reduces the friction. Further reduction can be achieved by installing a set of "turning vanes."

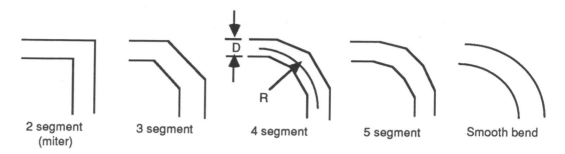

| 2 segment (miter) | 3 segment | 4 segment | 5 segment | Smooth bend |

The following table shows the pressure drop (in air flowing turbulently in a circular-cross-section duct) produced by 90-degree bend having 3, 4, or 5 segments in the elbow and having a variety of radius-of-curvature-of-centerline values. The ratio R/D is the ratio of the radius of curvature of the elbow centerline to the diameter of the duct.

Pressure drop in terms of length, in pipe diameters,
of straight duct (of same diameter) that has same pressure drop

Ratio: R/D	1	1.5	2	3	4	5	6
3-segment elbow	21	17	16	17	18	18	19
4-segment elbow	19	14	12	11	10	10	10
5-segment elbow (or smooth elbow)	16	12	10	7	6	5	4

Note: for 2-segment elbow (miter elbow) the pressure drop is 65 pipe diameters.

Example: What is the pressure drop in a 4-segment 90-deg elbow in a 4-in.-diameter duct system if the radius of curvature of the elbow centerline is 16 in? Answer: Noting that the R/D ratio is 4 and referring to the 5th column of the table, one sees that for a 4-segment elbow the value is 10 duct diameters, that is, 40 in.

PRESSURE DROP IN TURBULENT AIRFLOW IN A LONG, STRAIGHT DUCT OF RETANGULAR CROSS SECTION

To predict the pressure drop associated with turbulent airflow in a long straight duct that has rectangular cross section, one usually starts off by finding the equivalent circular-cross-section duct and then refers to the tables pertinent to circular-cross-section ducts. Experience shows, for example, that a duct of 8 x 12 in. cross section performs the same way a circular-cross-section duct of 10.7 in. diameter performs. Other correspondences are indicated below.

These rectangular ducts					correspond to	these circular ducts				
3x4	3x5	3x6	3x8	3x10		3.8	4.2	4.6	5.2	5.7 diam
4x4	4x5	4x6	4x8	4x10		4.4	4.9	5.3	6.1	6.8
5x8	5x10	5x12	5x14	5x16		6.9	7.6	8.3	8.9	9.4
6x8	6x10	6x12	6x14	6x16		7.5	8.4	9.1	9.8	10.4
8x12	8x14	8x16	8x18	8x20		10.7	11.5	12.2	12.9	13.5
10x12	10x14	10x16	10x18	10x20		11.9	12.9	13.7	14.5	15.2

Formula Instead of using a table such as the above, one may use this formula:

$$d = (1.3 \text{ in.}) \left[\frac{\left(\frac{L \times W}{\text{in.}^2} \right)^{0.625}}{\left(\frac{L + W}{\text{in.}} \right)^{0.250}} \right]$$

where L and W are the length and width of the rectangular cross section and d is the diameter of the equivalent circular-cross-section duct.

CENTRIFUGAL BLOWERS: PRESSURES AND FLOWRATES PRODUCED

The table on the next page shows the approximate pressure heads and volume flowrates achieved by centrifugal type blowers of various power ratings and various rotational speeds.

A LAW OF BLOWER PERFORMANCE

Under some conditions of use of blowers that are producing turbulent airflow, this so-called law is approximately valid: To double the volume airflow, you must double the rotational speed of the blower, which quadruples the pressure head and requires eight times as much electrical power. Or, in different words: Volume airflow varies directly as the rotational speed, the pressure head varies as the square of the rotational speed, and the power supplied to the blower varies as the cube of the rotational speed. Under some circumstances this law is not applicable.

To provide a pressure of	and a flowrate of		use a		
0.5 in. water	750	cfm	1/6 HP blower at	900	rpm
	1000		1/4	1000	
	1300		1/2	1200	
	1750		1	1500	
1.0 in. water	600		1/6	1050	
	800		1/4	1100	
	1150		1/2	1300	
	1600		1	1550	
1.5 in. water	400		1/6	1300	
	700		1/4	1300	
	1000		1/2	1400	
	1500		1	1600	
2.0 in. water	200		1/6	1500	
	500		1/4	1500	
	900		1/2	1500	

Chapter 17
Air Distribution Strategies

Delivering fresh air to the house is only part of the task. Another part is to deliver it exactly where it is needed, when needed. A very small exchanger may be mounted directly on an outside wall of the living room, bathroom, or other room. Larger exchangers are usually installed just below the floor or above the ceiling or in a utility room.

The exchanger should be located close to an outside wall, so that the fresh-air intake duct can be short. If it is short (and of course, well insulated), the fresh air entering the exchanger will be nearly as cold as outdoor air, and accordingly will be very effective at extracting heat from the outgoing air.

Before choosing the location, the architect or homeowner should consider carefully just where fresh air is most needed.

LOCATIONS OF OUTDOOR ENDS
OF INTAKE AND EXHAUST DUCTS

The outdoor ends of the ducts may be only a few feet apart, or may be 10 or more feet apart. The farther apart, the smaller the chance that some of the exhaust air will find its way back to the intake duct. If there is some nearby, outdoor source of pollution, the intake duct should be situated as far from this source as possible.

If the outdoor ends of the ducts are equipped with downward-turned terminal elbows or suitable hoods, rain and snow will be excluded. In snowy locations the duct ends should be situated at least 2 ft above ground level, to avoid blockage by deep snow.

If the duct ends are on the same side of the house, wind pressure will affect intake and exhaust ducts equally and so will not disturb the overall balance of airflows. If the intake duct is on the south side of the house, the intake air may be slightly warmed by solar radiation, which is helpful in winter.

INDOOR DISTRIBUTION STRATEGIES

No-Duct Distribution

Many exchangers are of small capacity, are mounted directly on an exterior wall, and employ no ducts. Fresh air from the exchanger flows directly into the room; usually this air emerges from the lower part of the exchanger and spreads outward and somewhat downward from the exchanger. Being somewhat colder than room air, the incoming air tends to descend toward the floor—accordingly the room occupants feel no current of cold air past their faces. Stale air is taken in by the exchanger via a grill in the upper part of the exchanger.

How much of the fresh air will reach kitchen, bathrooms, bedrooms? The answer may be *much* or *little* depending on how far away these rooms are and whether there are intervening closed doors.

How is the stale air collected by the exchanger? Collection is passive—and uncertain and delayed. Whatever pollutants diffuse to the neighborhood of the exchanger may be expelled to outdoors; other quantities of pollutants may remain in the house for long periods.

Some users purchase two exchangers and install them in two different rooms: the living room and one other room, say the master bedroom.

Distribution Using Ducts

Ofter ducts are used, especially if the exchanger's capacity is large—larger than is needed for just a living room.

There is this difficulty in making a choice: Should the duct system serve the fresh air, i.e., serve the delivery of air, or should it serve the stale air, i.e., serve the collection and expulsion of air? Or should there be two duct systems, one for fresh air and one for stale air?

Ducts used to deliver fresh air. Usually, the duct system is employed for delivery of fresh air *if the house already has a duct system*, e.g., for blower-forced delivery of hot air from a hot-air furnace or for blower-forced delivery (in summer) of cool air from a central air-cooler. The reasoning is simple: The duct system is already in place and is already delivering air to the rooms; put it to the additional use of distributing fresh air from the exchanger. When the hot-air-furnace blower is operating, it insures quick delivery of fresh air to many rooms; when the blower is *not* running, the delivery of fresh air continues because of the continual operation of the blowers within the exchanger.

The fresh air from the exchanger is normally introduced (to the furnace duct system) just upstream from the furnace; thus the fresh air is heated by passage through the furnace plenums and, before entering the rooms, is as hot as may desired.

Some *drawbacks* to this system are: (1) If airflow to some rooms has been shut off (by dampers), those rooms will receive no fresh air; even although a room may not need heat, it may need fresh air. (2) The powerful hot-air-furnace blower may create imbalance of the two air-flows in the exchanger: that blower tends to speed up the flow of incoming air but does not speed up the flow of outgoing air. (3) Elimination of polluted air from kitchen, bathroom, etc., is uncertain and delayed.

Ducts used to collect stale air. This strategy has the great merit that the most highly polluted air (for example, in kitchen and bathrooms) is collected immediately and locally. It is not given a chance to (or invited and encouraged to) diffuse into the other rooms prior to being collected and expelled. Fresh air may be delivered to one location (in living room, say) and permitted to diffuse into the other rooms. (Flow to other rooms may be negligible if the doors to those rooms are shut.) The ducts that carry the stale air to the exchanger do not need to be insulated.

Two-duct systems. Use of two-duct systems, one to collect stale air and the other to deliver fresh air, can sometimes be worthwhile. Usually, however, one duct system is enough.

WHERE, EXACTLY, IS FRESH AIR MOST NEEDED?

The answer depends on the location of the house (the kind of earth it rests on, the direction of the prevailing wind), the size and shape of the house, the materials used in construction, the kinds of uses to which the rooms are put and the locations of the rooms, the extent to which the rooms are isolated from one another by walls and closed doors, the types of stove and furnace, the habits of the occupants (number of long showers taken, number of persons smoking, frequency with which cooking of cabbages, broccoli, and other oderiferous forms of food occurs, any hobbies that involve release of pollutants), and any special health problems (especially pulmonary problems) the occupants have.

Some Pertinent Questions

Kitchen	Gas stove?
	Much used?
	Much cooking of smelly vegetables?
	Does kitchen have its own air-exhaust system?
	Is this put to use frequently?
	Window often left partly open?
Bathroom	Much used?
	Long showers?
	Does bathroom have its own air-exhaust system?
	Is this put to use frequently?
	Window often left partly open?
Living room	Much used?
	Much smoking?
	Many sofas, chairs, rugs, etc., that contain formaldehyde?
Bedrooms	Many materials that contain formaldehyde?
	Windows left open all night?
Basement or crawl-space	Damp?
	Gas furnace? Oil furnace?
	Leaky oil tank?
	Does earth beneath basement contain much radon-emitting material? Is the terrain granitic?
	Does basement have a floor that is impervious to radon?

Is house very airtight?
Are vapor barriers used? Just in outer walls? In ceiling also?
Between first-story floor and basement? Between basement and earth beneath it?
Has urea formaldehyde insulation been used?
Is the house in a windy location?

INSULATION, SCREENS, AND DAMPERS
FOR DUCTS RUNNING TO OUTDOORS

The ducts running between the exchanger and the outdoors are very cold in winter and should be insulated—not only to minimize heat-loss to them but also to reduce the likelihood that moisture will condense on them. The cold-air intake duct is especially cold and its insulation should be covered by a vapor barrier and this should be well sealed.

Both of the outdoor duct-ends should be equipped with screens that will exclude animals, flies, bees, etc.

If the exchanger is to be left *off* for long periods in winter, backdraft dampers should be installed. Otherwise, cold air can find its way into the rooms via the (inoperative) exchanger.

Chapter 18
Sensors, Controls, and Installation

How is the rate of supply of fresh air to be controlled? Manually? Or automatically? If automatic control is used, what parameter should it be based on and what kind of sensor should be used? What happens if the device fails, or the electric power fails? Is some kind of failure indicator needed? Is some kind of *automatic correction* of failure, or crude compensation for failure, needed?

MANUAL CONTROL

Obviously an exchanger can be controlled manually: it can be turned on or off, or changed from low speed to high speed, by a member of the household. This approach is simple and inexpensive, but if the members of the household are careless or forgetful, performance may be poor: not enough fresh air sometimes, too much (with consequent waste of heat) at other times. Also, the need to keep the exchanger in mind and the need to make decisions as to whether to change the switch setting may prove to be a burden.

Besides changing the speed of the exchanger, the members of the household may adjust dampers so as to redistribute the fresh air (or removal of stale air) in different parts of the house at different times of day. They can focus on the living room during the day and the bedrooms at night, for example.

CONTROL BY TIMER

A device that contains an electric clock may be employed to change the exchanger speed at different times of day. It could control, also, the dampers that govern the distribution of air to (or from) the rooms.

In choosing when to have the exchanger run at low speed, run at high speed, or remain off, the house occupant would, obviously, take account of the times at which showers are taken, the kitchen stove is in use, and other pollution-prone activities occur.

CONTROL BY TEMPERATURE

Using an outdoor thermometer, one might arrange to reduce blower-power whenever the outdoor temperature is below, say, 30°F. This would save some money, inasmuch as the exchanger's efficiency is well below 100% and thus significant loss of heat occurs whenever the outdoor temperature is very low. It makes good sense to be generous with fresh air on warm days and stingy on very cold days. Also, reducing the speed of exchanger operation on very cold days may be permissible inasmuch as natural infiltration is then at a maximum, thanks to chimney effect.

Some exchanger manufacturers supply a temperature sensor that is used to sense the threat of air-blockage by frost. When there is partial blockage of the outgoing-air passages, the incoming air entering the room is colder than it normally is; a thermometer that detects this situation can take constructive action, such as slowing or temporarily stopping the blower driving the incoming fresh air. Alternatively, the temperature sensor can be placed in the stream of stale air being discharged from the exchanger; whenever this air is colder than 32°F, with a resulting threat of frost formation, the sensor can turn off the blower driving the incoming fresh air.

CONTROL BY HUMIDITY

A humidistat (or dehumidistat) may be used to turn on an exchanger, or change the speed from low to high, whenever the relative humidity of room air exceeds a certain value, say 50%. (This remark applies, obviously, to exchangers that do not recover water. It applies also, but to a lesser extent, to exchangers that *do* recover water, inasmuch as the recovery is far less than 100%.)

Several exchanger manufacturers recommend use of a dehumidistat. The general assumption, which is not always valid, is that whenever there is no need to reduce humidity, there is no need to operate the exchanger.

CONTROL BY CONCENTRATION OF POLLUTANT

Ideally, the rooms would include a set of sensors, each responsive to a different major pollutant, and each capable of turning on the exchanger (or increasing its speed of operation) whenever a pollutant-concentration is found to exceed a specified limit. This approach might be practical with respect to a few pollutants—in certain special situations existing today, e.g., a large and important buiding containing many people, with a known serious pollution threat. Perhaps the practicality will be widespread in another 10 or 20 years.

CONTROL BY ACTIVATION OF A HOUSEHOLD UTILITY

Arrangement can be made whereby the exchanger is turned on, or turned up, whenever a bathroom door is closed, or a cooking stove is activated, or a clothes dryer is activated, or electric power is turned on in a workshop or hobby room.

THE "CONSTANT ON" ALTERNATIVE

At least one manufacturer of exchangers recommends keeping the exchanger running at all times, or all times throughout the winter. Why? Because this insures a good supply of fresh air at all times. Never will the exchanger be turned off (say by an improperly set temperature or humidity sensor) at an inappropriate time. Never will the house occupants turn it off manually for some trivial reason—and forget to turn it on again. A study made by the Washington State Energy Office showed a surprising and alarming tendency for exchangers to be off when they should be on. A majority of the occupants reported that their exchangers operated seldom or hardly at all.

DEFROSTING

Accumulation of frost can cause serious trouble, especially in exchangers of fixed-plate type. The frost can reduce, and eventually entirely stop, the outflow of stale air. Cold air may continue to flow into the house—there is no tendency for passages for incoming air to accumulate ice—even after the outgoing airflow has been stopped. One result is that the passages for outgoing air receive no further heat from the rooms; they become even colder and become locked into freezing condition. Another result is that the incoming air, no longer receiving any heat, enters the rooms while extremely cold and may produce much discomfort. A third result is that stale air tends to accumulate within the rooms.

How can this difficulty be overcome? There are several approaches: Manually turn off the air-inflow blower when frosting begins. Then there is no further cooling of exchanger components, and even a reduced flow of outgoing warm air will eventually melt the frost and make the passages clear again. Manually or automatically turn off the air-inflow blower for 10 minutes (say) out of every hour. Such intervals of no cold air inflow will allow the frost to be melted.

Arrange for automatic turn-off of the air-inflow blower whenever the frost accumulation reaches a certain dangerous amount. In other words, turn off that blower only when a definite problem exists. Control may be provided by a temperature sensor that finds the temperature of the stale air leaving the room to be abnormally low: below 32°F, for example. Or control can be provided by a pressure gauge that finds the pressure produced by the stale air outflow blower to be abnormally high, as as consequence of blockage of the outgoing air passages.

Arrange for a small electric heater to be energized and reduce the frosting. The heater may be placed in either airstream, at a location upstream from the location where frost formation starts.

Various manufacturers have adopted different recommendations, or have provided different auxiliary equipment, to accomplish defrosting.

Notice that all of the procedures mentioned above imply a loss of heat. Although much latent heat is converted to sensible heat when ice is formed, an equivalent amount of sensible heat is required to melt the ice. Thus there is no net benefit derived from the heat associated with the production of ice. (I have invented a scheme that, in principle, would make almost full benefit of this heat; but whether the scheme is practicable is not known.)

INVERSE-OF-WINDSPEED CONTROL

There is obvious merit in the idea of having the speed of the exchanger blower diminish as the outdoor windspeed increases. Every house has some natural infiltration, and this increases with windspeed. What is important, in keeping levels of pollution low, is the total rate of fresh-air input: the greater the natural input, the smaller the input needed from the exchanger. (If the house occupant ignores this, he will be wasting heat and electrical power whenever the windspeed is great.)

It would not be difficult to employ an above-roof-mounted hot-wire anemometer and arrange for the output signal to reduce blower power as the windspeed increases. At some very high windspeed, say 25 mph, the exchanger should be shut off entirely, in certain not extremely tight houses.

Note: I have elsewhere described a passive type of "inverse vent": a house vent which would automatically and passively gradually close as windspeed increases, so that the overall rate of air change (via cracks, etc., and via the special vent) would remain constant. Clearly such a device would slightly reduce the need for an air-to-air heat-exchanger.

CONTROL FOR ENCOURAGING CONDENSATION
OF MOISTURE BUT PREVENTING FROST ACCUMULATION

Perhaps it would be feasible to provide a control that would regulate airflow rates (or regulate preheating or some other parameter) in such a way that, under typical conditions in very cold weather, within-exchanger condensation of moisture would occur but no frost would accumulate.

The process of condensation may be welcomed if it leads to some recovery of latent heat, but the process of frost formation may be most unwelcome. The line between condensate formation and frost formation may be a narrow one, yet it might be feasible to design a control that would encourage operation that comes close to the line but does not cross it!

DEVICES FOR WARNING OF POWER LOSS OR EXCHANGER FAILURE

Suppose that the exchanger routinely used in a very tight house fails: a blower motor fails, the electric supply fails, the air passages become completely blocked, or some other misadventure befalls. Will the house-occupants remain unaware of such failure? Will the concentrations of pollutants build up indefinitely? Will the health of the occupants be impaired?

One may expect that, ordinarily, no harm will result. The pollutant concentrations will not be so very excessive; the occupants may notice the build-up of smells or humidity; they may notice that the noise of the blowers has ceased; they may notice that the entire house is without electric power. Thus they may take suitable steps, such as opening a window or quitting the house.

But the designer must expect that failure of the exchanger may indeed occur. He may feel obliged to provide some equipment that, at the least, will warn the occupants that there is trouble.

Such trouble could be sensed by a device that detects a drop in voltage or detects a drop in air pressure close downstream from a blower.

Visual Devices

Whenever the exchanger is operating, a green light may be lit to show that operation is proceeding smoothly. If the light goes out, the occupants should take action. (But will they notice that the light goes out? Perhaps they are in another room, or are asleep.)

Alternatively, a very bright light might be turned on automatically whenever the general electric supply fails. The bright-light bulb would be energized by a battery. (But might not the battery be dead when the time comes for it to do its duty? And might not the bright light be unnoticed, if the occupants are asleep or in a different room?)

A manometer connected so as to indicate the pressure drop across the heat exchanger proper would give helpful information, e.g., information as to blower failure or clogging of the outgoing-air passages by dust or frost.

Ribbons hung in the fresh-air stream emerging from the exchanger might do nearly as good a job. If the ribbons stop moving, no fresh air is coming in!

Audible Devices

Battery-operated buzzers, bells, or the like might be used to indicate loss of power. However, such systems may be ineffective if the occupants are deaf, or are in a remote room, of if the batteries are dead.

INSTALLATION

Although various small exchangers are designed for installation directly in an external wall, most exchangers are installed in a utility room, or in a basement (close beneath the ceiling), or in an attic.

Use of a vibration-absorbing suspension is desirable, and sound-absorbing segments (sleeves) may be included in the ducts that connect the exchanger to room grilles.

The ducts connecting the exchanger to the outdoors must be insulated and should be kept short; that is, the exchanger should be situated as close as convenient to the chosen outdoor wall.

The outdoor ends of ducts should be equipped with hoods to exclude rain and snow and should be fitted with fly screens.

Several ducts may be used to carry stale air from bathrooms, kitchen, etc., to the exchanger. The warmed fresh air may be delivered, by a duct, to a central location (hallway or living room) and allowed to diffuse naturally to other rooms; or several ducts may be used to insure delivery to all important rooms. Such air is usually delivered at a near-ceiling location, so that, as it descends, it will mix with the warmer room air and will cause no discomfort. The discharge location should be kept distant from locations of favorite armchairs, etc.

Dampers may be installed to permit changing the distribution of fresh air to the various rooms.

To avoid back pressures that will slow the airflows, the designer should minimize the lengths of ducts, have few (or no) sharp bends, and should use ducts of generous diameter.

Most manufacturers' brochures contain valuable advice on installation strategies.

BALANCING

Usually the rates of flow of stale air and fresh air should be equal, that is, balanced. When the two airstreams are balanced, the air to air heat exchanger performs especially well. If the outflow of stale air exceeds the inflow of fresh air, the house will be at lower pressure than the outdoor air, and the inflow of cold outdoor air through cracks, etc., will be increased. Also, there may be a tendency for smoke within a chimney to be sucked back into the house—a condition (called backdrafting) that is highly undesirable. If the inflow of fresh air exceeds the outflow of stale air, the incoming air will be warmed by the exchanger to a reduced extent only; discomfort will be experienced and more back-up heat will be needed.

Achieving balance is not easy, especially since it may be disturbed by changes in direction and speed of wind, by operation of bathroom and kitchen exhaust fans, by the opening of a window, by operation of a hot-air furnace, and other factors. In very cold weather, the chimney effect within the exchanger ducts can slightly spoil balance.

The commonest ways of balancing the two airstreams are (1) slightly change the amount of electrical power supplied to one of the blower motors, or (2) partially close a damper in one of the ducts until balance is achieved. To see whether balance exists, close all windows, outside doors, fireplace dampers, etc., then open a living room window an inch and, with the aid of a puff of smoke or a dangling thread, see that no inflow or outflow of air occurs here. Another procedure is to employ a flowmeter that can be inserted in a duct path; insert it successively in the two airstreams and see that the flowrates are equal.

Some installers of exchangers carefully balance the flows before calling the installation complete, and some exchanger manufacturers provide "self-balancing" accessories.

Chapter 19

Commercially Available Air-To-Air Heat Exchangers

Summarized below is technical and price information on major types of air-to-air heat-exchangers widely available in the United States and Canada. The information includes in most cases names, model numbers, flowrates, dimensions, prices, and also the names, addresses, and telephone numbers of the manufacturers.

Small sketches suggest the shape of the device and the arrangement of internal components. Because designs, prices, etc., are changed so frequently, readers cannot rely on the data give here but should contact the manufacturers or their distributors for the latest information.

In some instances, the word "efficiency" may appear where the correct word is "effectiveness." The recently adopted terminology is not yet fully understood by writers inside and outside of the manufacturing companies.

Appended to this chapter are concise summaries of the exchanger manufacturers, types, prices, etc., and an index of trade names.

ACS-Hoval

955 North Lively Blvd., Wood Dale IL 60191   (312) 860-6800.

This company is a division of Air Distribution Associates, Inc., which has the same address. The company makes two kinds of equipment: one for large buildings (office buildings, restaurants, schools, etc.) and one for houses.

Equipment for large buildings. There are two main models produced. **Model N** has core edges horizontal and vertical. In **Model D**, most of the core edges are at 45 deg. Within each model there are many series, called 30, 60, 70, 85 and the "doubled" series 120, 140, and 170—this set provides airflows of 50 to 50,000 cfm. Efficiencies vary widely, depending on static pressure head and flow rate chosen. Claimed typical efficiency: 60 to 90%. Typical static pressures: 0.03 to 2 in. H_2O.

Exchanger cores, of crossflow type, employ dimpled aluminum plates double-folded at the edges for airtightness. In all there are 7 sizes of plates and 53 standard lengths of core. Some models employ multiple cores.

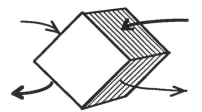

Single-stack crossflow core mounted at 45°

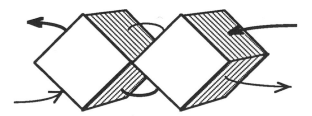

Core consisting of two stacks in counterflow-crossflow arrangement

No filters are provided, but full provisions for cleaning (and in many models, washing) are included. Housings are of aluminum. No blowers are included, and no controls—but of course these can be procured separately.

PB models. A special series called PB is supplied complete with two blowers, a supply-air filter, and *wash* provision. The six types, called PB-51, PB-52, PB-53, PB-54, PB-55, PB-56, provide flowrates from 1,600 to 34,000 cfm. A great variety of accessories and options are vailable.

Equipment for houses. The company has recently branched out to produce "PC" models designed for use in houses. These models are of combined counterflow-crossflow type, employing two aluminum plate cores in series within an insulated aluminum housing. There are two motors, two blowers, automatic defrost, and 6-in. duct connections.

Overall length, height, and width are 46.75 x 17.5 x 12.25 in. for the standard efficiency models and 66.5 x 17.5 x 12.25 for the high-efficiency models. The respective weights are 46 lb and 66 lb.

Options include filters, humidistat control, remote on/off switch, mounting kit, and many others.

Model	Flowrate (cfm)	Max overall power (W)	Efficiency	Trade price
PC-130-140	110-160	240	52-65%	$635
PC-230-140	110-160	240	68-85%	$855
PC-130-250	215-285	426	52-65%	$785
PC-230-250	215-285	426	68-85%	$1,005

Air Changer Marketing

1297 Industrial Rd., Cambridge, Ontario, Canada N3H 4T8 (519) 653-7129.

Distributes equipment made by Clawsey-Sohrt Mfg. Co. Ltd. Earlier equipment was made by Air Changer Co. Ltd., owned for a while by Nortron Industries Ltd. Original design was by Allen-Drerup-White Ltd.

Markets Air Changer Series 2000 air-to-air heat-exchangers. No one or two standard and complete pieces of equipment are available. Instead a great variety of modules, or components, are available: core assemblies, air-moving and control assemblies, and optional accessories.

Standard core assemblies

CC6 50x15x25 in. The core, of plastic copolymer, has 280 ft^2 of heat-transfer area. The housing is of baked-enamel-coated steel. A filter for the stale air stream is included. Weight: 104 lb. List price: $435 US.

CC6S As above, except shorter (30 in.), lighter (60 lb.), with a smaller heat-transfer area (130 ft^2), and cheaper ($335 US).

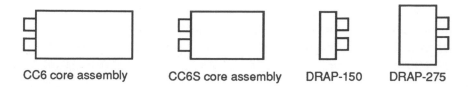

| CC6 core assembly | CC6S core assembly | DRAP-150 | DRAP-275 |

Air-moving and control assemblies

DRAP-150 Two motors, two axial fans, automatic and manual remote 2-speed control, 2-speed integral direct-reading dehumidistat, automatic demand defrost. 22lb. $390 US.

Model **DSP-150** is similar except that it has only a single speed and Model **SP-150** has a single speed and lacks the defrost capability. The respective list prices are $340 and $240 US.

DRAP-275 Like DRAP-150 but employs blowers and provides about twice the flowrate. Also it has an electronic airflow balancing system, operative during low-speed operation only. It is heavier (62 lb.) and costs more ($595 US, list).

Models **DSP-275** and **SP-275** also have higher flowrate and also have the limitations of the above-mentioned DSP-150 and SP-150 models; list prices are $540 and $445 US respectively.

A complete system consisting of the **CC6** core assembly and the **DRAP-150** attached box provides, under typical conditions, flowrates of 50 and 120 cfm with efficiencies of 82% and 76% . Electrical power: about 80 W.

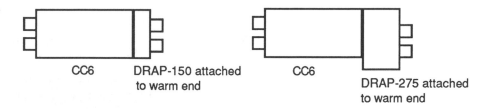

| CC6 | DRAP-150 attached to warm end | CC6 | DRAP-275 attached to warm end |

A complete system consisting of the **CC6** core assembly and the **DRAP-275** attached box provides, under typical conditions, flowrates of 120 and 200 cfm with efficiencies of 80% and 76%. Electrical power using low speed is 120 W, and using high speed is 260 W. Accessory options include: pressure balance kit, motorized damper, outside vent hood, 30-minute crank timer for bathroom or kitchen, remote dehumidistat, silencer.

Air Distribution Associates Inc. (see ACS-Hoval).

AirXchange Inc.

401 V. F. W. Drive, Rockland MA 02370 (617) 871-4816.

Manufactures several models of rotary-type air-to-air heat exchangers. In 1987 the exchangers were distributed by Nutone, but starting in 1988 AirXchange itself handled distribution.

Model 502CA. This is the standard model meant for use in not-too-cold climates and intended to serve houses of moderate to generous size. It is designed to be mounted horizontally in an interior location (ceiling, wall, floor, utility room, or basement).

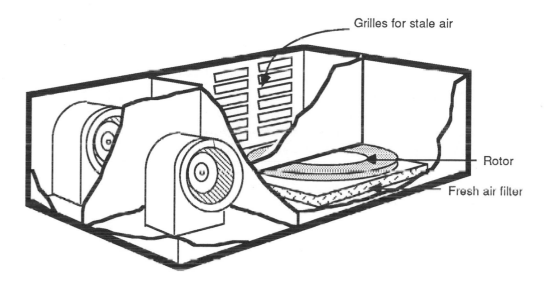

The core consists of a rotor 16 in. in diameter and 0.75 in. thick. It is constructed of a 0.005-in.-thick ribbon of oriented polystyrene wound at the rate of 52 layers per in., with 0.014-in. airspaces between layers. Thus the pathlength of airflow through the rotor is 0.75 in., and the total heat-transfer area is 100 sq ft. The rotor surfaces are desiccant-coated so as to provide some transfer of moisture from one airstream to the other, and thus permit only a moderate net outflow of moisture on dry, cold winter days and a moderate net inflow of moisture on humid summer days.

The rotor lies in a horizontal plane, rotating about a vertical axis at 15 rpm so that any given sector is traversed by warm air for 2 sec, then by cold air for 2 sec, etc. Thus the cycle time for exchange of heat and moisture is 4 sec. The rotor is easily removable, as for manual cleaning. (In fact cleaning is largely automatic and continual, thanks to the rapid reversals of airflow direction.)

A single 150 w motor drives two centrifugal blowers, all mounted on a single shaft, driving the two (stale air, fresh air) airflows at the same rate: nominally 150 cfm (low speed) or 200 cfm (high speed). Choice of speed (high, low, off) is controlled by a manually operated switch.

Fresh air is drawn upward through a filter and through one half of the rotor and rotor chamber, and stale air flows downward through the other half. Vertical metal separator plates keep the two airstreams from intermingling; cross leakage is about 5%. Ducts carry the input fresh air and the output fresh air, and a duct carries the output stale air to the outdoors. Stale air input to the exchanger is via grilles in the housing; no duct is needed ordinarily, but a duct may be installed where necessary.

There is no drain. Ordinarily, any moisture condensed from the outgoing stale air is immediately vaporized into the (cold, dry) incoming fresh air. Also there is no dehumidistat or defrost system. Ducts are not included.

The housing, of "galvalume" coated steel, is 29.25 x 17.38 x 10.25 in. It is insulated with fiberglass and foam plastic. Overall weight of the exchanger: 44 lb. Heat-recovery efficiency: 77% (HVI certified). The system is especially well suited to direct connection to a forced air heating or air cooling installation, with resultant savings on ducting, etc. Suggested retail price: $619.

Main option: A preheat frost control system (required in very cold climates) that includes a sensor of outdoor temperature and an in-duct electric preheater of incoming cold air. The sensor controls the rate of heating (up to 1500 w in Model PH-1500, up to 3000 w in Model PH-3000) so that the fresh air entering the room will have a specified comfort temperature. Other options: Dehumidistat, to maintain room-air relative humidity at a selected value. Ducts. Duct caps.

Model 502NDC-L. This model, for use in very cold climates, is similar to Model 502CA but employs (as standard equipment) a frost control system that is far simpler than the above-described preheat frost control system. However, when the outdoor temperature falls below 5°F (-15° C), the performance is less versatile and the operating cost is higher; specifically the stale-air-exhaust rate is limited to 70 cfm, and the fresh air intake duct is entirely closed off by a damper; thus, there is no heat recovery and the house receives fresh air by general infiltration only. Suggested list price of model, complete with damper defrost control: $700.

Model 502CW. Same as Model 502CA but intended for use in not-very-cold climates. The rotor is not desiccant-coated; thus, wintertime reduction of indoor humidity is enhanced. Price: $578.

Model 570. This standard model, smaller than the Model 502 series, is meant for use in houses or apartments of small or moderate size and is designed for mounting on an external wall or window. No ducts needed. The design is much like that of the Model 502, but differs in these respects: Smaller (23.13 x 14.13 x 11 in.). 25 lb. Smaller rotor, with 35 sq ft transfer area. Smaller motor and blowers, providing 30 to 70 cfm, with 45 to 55 w electric power consumption. Mounted with long axis horizontal or vertical, in window opening or in special hole cut in external wall. There is no defrost system, no dehumidistat, no drain. The rotor is not desiccant-coated. Price: $498.

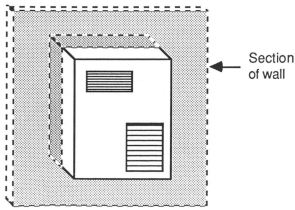

Section of wall

Model 570N. Same as above except includes automatic motor-operated damper that prevents frosting in the manner described in a previous paragraph. Price: $578.

Model 570D. Same as Model 570 except designed for ceiling mount. Ducts required. Price: $438.

Model 570ND. Same as Model 570D except an automatic damper for frost-control is included. Price: $518.

American Aldes Ventilation Corp.

Northgate Center Industrial Park, 4539 Northgate Court, Sarasota Fl 33580 (813) 351-3441.

Distributes the **VMP-H** exchanger developed and manufactured in France. The core, of crossflow type, includes polyvinyl chloride plates having a total heat-transfer area of 160 ft^2. The steel housing is 38.5 x 20.5 x 11.5 in. and contains 14 cutouts for ducts. Weight of core assembly: 22 lb. Efficiency (at 90 cfm) 70%. No blowers, filters, or controls are included.

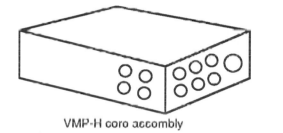

VMP-H core assembly

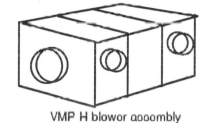

VMP H blower assembly

The blower system, which includes one 1200/1800 rpm motor and two squirrel-cage impellors, has the dimensions 16 x 15 x 12 in. Total airflow of stale air is 85 cfm during low-speed operation and 130 to 160 cfm during high-speed operation; for the fresh air flow the rates are 85 and 130 cfm. Typical power levels during low-speed and high-speed operation are about 100 W and 200 W. A complete system includes a two-speed control and other components. List price: $1,000.

Many accessories are available. For example, flexible ducts for carrying stale air from kitchen, bathroom, etc., to the core assembly, and other ducts to carry fresh air to living room, dining room, bedrooms, etc., Several kinds of vents and outlets are available. Defrost system. Cores of aluminum. List price of a kit that includes ducts, duct fittings, and defrost system is about $1,500.

The company markets two unique devices for controlling the rate of ventilation of an individual room even when the blowers of the main system continue to operate at constant speed. One device is a VMP-K air inlet port of responsive type. The other is a "Hygro" air outlet port of responsive type.

VMP-K air inlet port. This device, intended to admit fresh air to a bedroom, for example, contains a variable-size aperture that becomes smaller when the room-air underpressure increases and becomes larger when the underpressure decreases. Thus the rate of fresh air inflow remains practically constant irrespective of underpressure changes—changes produced, for example, by changes in inlet apertures in other rooms.

Principle of operation: a rubber bulb is situated at the center of an aperture, partially blocking it, and the bulb cross-section changes as the bulb tends to inflate or deflate under the influence of a tiny airstream controlled by room-air underpressure.

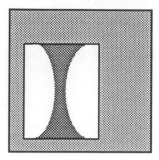 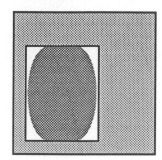

Hygro air outlet port. This device is designed to regulate the discharge of stale air from, say, a kitchen in which large increases in humidity occasionally threaten to occur. The Hygro device includes a variable aperture the area of which increases when the relative humidity of the room air increases, and vice versa. A rubber bulb is employed, and becomes smaller when an inflating airstream is reduced by a humidity sensor.

Usually the Hygro air outlet port is used with the VMP-K air inlet port. List price of a simple VMP system that includes blowers, housing, and the VMP-K air inlet port is about $300.

Aston Industries Inc.
PO Box 220, St. Leonard d'Aston, Quebec, Canada JOC 1MO   (819) 399-2175.

The company makes a complete exchanger (Thermatube 2300 and fresh-air blower plus stale-air blower system). The company also makes aluminum crossflow cores for various original equipment manufacturers.

Thermatube 2300 and fresh-air blower. Thermatube proper includes a core proper, a housing, and a blower. The core consists of 26 glass tubes each 48 in. long and 1.25 in. diameter, arranged in a horizontal array with air spaces between tubes. They carry the stale air. Fresh air flows outside the tubes, following a zig-zag path governed by baffles. Heat transfer area: 34 ft^2.

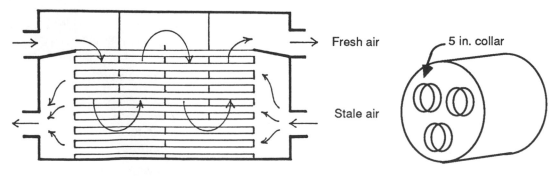

Thermatube 2300 core and housing. Highly schematic longitudinal cross section showing only a few of the 26 glass tubes.

Stale air blower system

The blower drives the fresh air. The 57 x 25 x 8 in. housing is made of polystyrene foam covered by a sheet of vinvl plastic. At each end there are two 5-in. diameter steel collars. The one that serves the stale air entering the core contains a filter. Retail cost range: $250 to $300 US.

There are two choices of *stale-air blower system*: Conformax CM-D, intended for use by contractors, and Aston Atic 2000, intended for use by homeowners.

The Conformax CM-D, with length 12 in. and diameter 13 in., contains a single blower that receives stale air from kitchen, bathroom, etc., and delivers this air to the Thermatube 2300 core and thence to the outdoors, at a flowrate of up to 150 cfm. Blower power 160 W. Retail cost range: $250 to $300 US.

The Aston Atic 2000, shipped as a kit for homeowners, is much like the Conformax CM-D but has a rectangular shape. Overall cost of entire system, including essential fittings etc.: $600 to $900 US.

Berner International Corp.
PO Box 5205, New Castle PA 16105 (412) 658-3551.

Many years ago the company made many types of large exchangers for use in industry, etc., and distributed a few models for use in houses. Currently it concentrates on exchangers for houses. Three types are marketed.

EM-120, designed to be mounted on the wall of living room or other room. It includes one motor, two air impellors, and a plastic (teflon-base) rotor 9 in. diameter and 2.6 in. thick. The rotor is desiccant-coated and so provides a moderate extent of moisture recovery. Flowrates are 30 to 55 cfm. Power usage is 25 to 40 W. Dimensions: 21.5 x 12.5 x 8 in. Weight: 21 lb. Efficiency: 75 to 82%. Retail price: $390.

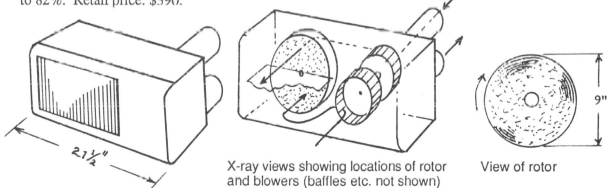

X-ray views showing locations of rotor and blowers (baffles etc. not shown)   View of rotor

Em-250, a larger version, with three speeds, provides 75 to 150 cfm with power usage of 70 to 120 W and efficiency of 70 to 75%. Dimensions: 31 x 28 x 14 in. Weight: 73 lb. Retail price: about $1,000.

EM-500, the largest version. With three speeds it provides 170 to 300 cfm with power usage of 90 to 260 W and efficiency of 71 to 80%. Dimensions: 40 x 28 x 14 in. Weight: 106 lb. Retail price: about $1,400.

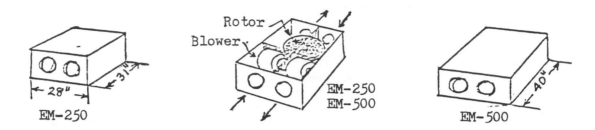

A model 1AQ that includes the capability of removing some noxious gases, pollen, etc., is to be available by late 1988.

Blackhawk Industries Inc.

607 Park St., Regina, Saskatchewan, Canada S4N 5N1   (306) 924-1551.

This company took over from Enercon Industries Inc. (and/or Enercon of America, Inc.) late in 1982. Initially it continued producing and selling exchangers such as Enercon had been making and selling. These were cylindrical models containing cylindrical heat-exchange sheets. In 1987 preparations were being made for producing an entirely new line of exchangers containing several sophisticated and versatile components.

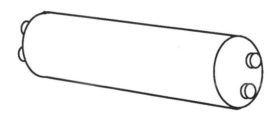

Bossaire

1321 Tyler St. NE, Minneapolis MN 55413   (612) 781-0179.

The company produces five models of air-to-air heat-exchanger, called BX-75, BX-125, BX-150, BX-250, BX-350. All are of approximately similar design, but of different size. The core is of aluminum plates spaced 0.14 in. apart; thus the heat-transfer area ranges from about 100 ft^2 in BX-75 to 760 ft^2 in BX-350.

The flow pattern is combined counterflow and crossflow; the two halves of the core are pneumatically in series (counterflow) and within each half the flow is crossflow. The housing, of galvanized steel, includes 1 inch of fiberglass. The front and back panels are removable, to permit easy cleaning of the core.

The two blowers and two blower motors are mounted in the upper part of the housing. Each operates on air that has already passed through the core and each runs at a single speed (there is no choice of high and low speed). The nominal flowrates range from 75 cfm for the BX-75 to 350 cfm for the BX-350.

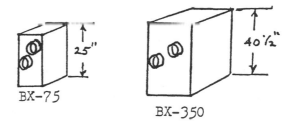

The overall power usages range from 120 W to about 310 W. The nominal effectiveness is 80%, and the efficiency is slightly less. Collar diameters range from 4 in. to 8 in. The overall dimensions range from 24.5 x 11.5 x 12 in. for BX-75 to 40 x 25.5 x 22 in. for BX-350. Weights range from 40 lb. to 125 lb.

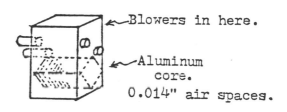

Automatic defrost (by stopping the inflow of fresh air) is initiated automatically when the emerging stale air cools below (for example) 38°F.

The exchangers are designed to serve houses with volumes of about 1,500, 2,500, 3,500, 5,500, and 8,000 ft^2. The list prices range from about $660 to about $1,500.

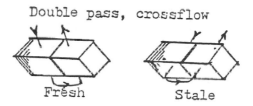

Double pass, crossflow

Fresh   Stale

Conservation Energy Systems Inc.

3310 Millar Ave., Saskatoon, Saskatchewan, Canada S7K 7G9 (306) 242-3663.
US distributor: Conservation Energy Systems Inc. Box 10116, Minneapolis MN 55458 (800) 667-3717.

Produces VanEE heat-exchanger models 1000, 2000, and 7000 and also a variety of major accessories.

VanEE Model 1000 basic. This small, simple exchanger, designed for small houses, mobile homes, etc., employs a crossflow polypropylene core. A single motor drives two centrifugal blowers. These produce airflows of 100 cfm against 0.2 in. static pressure. Efficiency: about 70%. The housing, with dimensions 25 x 21 x 13 in., is of 22-gauge galvanized steel with an enamel coating. It is insulated with foil-faced fiberglass. Drain pans are of ABS plastic. Two permanent washable filters are included, as well as rubber fittings to reduce vibration and noise.

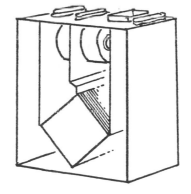

The collars serving the ducts that run to outdoors and require insulation are of double type to confine the insulation termination. The ducts are assumed to be of 5-inch and 6-inch diameters. The side panels of the housing are removable, to facilitate servicing.

Overall weight: 65 lb. No speed control, dehumidistat, timer, or defrost system is included. Suggested list price: $445 US.

The **Model 1000L** includes a 24-v remote control switch and variable speed drive. Price: $495 US.

The **Model 1000LD** includes a 24-v remote control switch, variable speed drive, and a Frostbuster automatic balanced-flow defrost system that performs essential service in climates more severe than 5,000°F degree days. The device occasionally (once every 51 minutes when the outdoor temperature is below 23°F) provides a 6-minute defrost cycle in which the stale-air blower is off, the fresh-air blower continues but drives room air, rather than outdoor air, thanks to the actions of a motorized damper that closes the fresh-air intake port and opens a special room-air port. Flow balance is maintained and no electrical preheating is involved. Price: $577.

VanEE Model 2000 Standard. This exchanger, intended to serve an entire house of typical or generous size, is much like the Model 1000 Basic but provides greater airflow and more versatile control. It is larger (34 x 21 x 17 in.), heavier (75 lb), includes two motors, provides 256 cfm airflows against 0.2 in. static pressure and 220 cfm against 0.4 in. static pressure. Efficiency: about 60 to 76% depending on flowrate. The equipment includes a 24-v remote control switch and variable speed drive. There is no defrost system, no dehumidistat, no electronic timer. Suggested list price: $660.

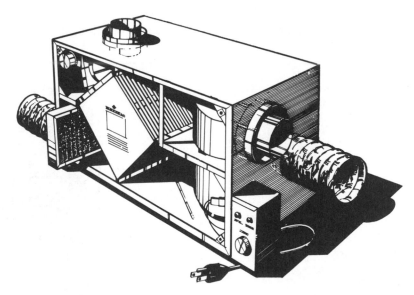

The **Model 2000SLD** includes a frostbuster defrost system. The suggested list price is $829. Options include remote dehumidistat, remote switches, timer controls, and zone control, ducts, screens, etc., screened intake and exhaust hoods, airflow indicator lights, dampers, and 1 and 2 kW electric heaters.

VanEE Model 7000 Series. Exchangers of this series are intended for very large houses, health spas, swimming pools, office buildings, etc. They are somewhat similar to the Model 2000 exchangers but are much larger (47 x 20 x 19 in.), much heavier (225 lb) , and provide much greater airflows: about 700 cfm against 0.2 in. static pressure and 600 cfm against 0.4 in. static pressure.

Suggested list prices range from $1,060 to $1,840. The latter price refers to models that include many major accessories, including a Frostbuster defrost system, remote dehumidistat control, and filters of 2-inch-thick pleated type.

Des Champs Laboratories Inc.

Box 440, 17 Farinella Dr., East Hanover, NJ 07936 (210) 884-1460.

Makes eight E-Z Vent (EZV) models: two for single room, six for whole house.

Single-room models

Model EZV-175A, for installation in attic or basement. Flowrate: 75 cfm. Weight: 30 lb. Efficiency: 75%. List price: $310. Model Ezv-175W, for through-wall installation: Specifications generally as above. A superior, deluxe, simulated woodgrain face plate is included. The price is higher: $340.

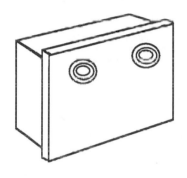

Whole-house models

Model EZV-210: The core consists of one continuous folded 0.006-inch-thick aluminum sheet, arranged for counterflow. Plate length: 24 in. Plate spacing: 0.22 inch. The blowers may be driven at either of two speeds. There is a washable, non-metallic filter in each airstream. The housing, of galvanized steel, is provided with one inch of Fiberflex insulation. There are two drains.

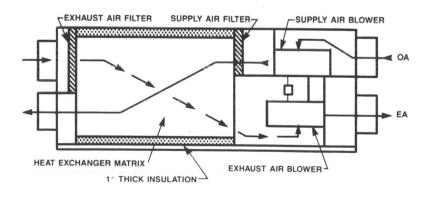

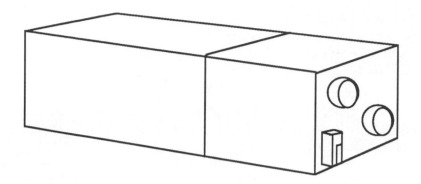

Collar diameter: 6 in. Overall dimensions: 46 x 18 x 14 in. Weight: 80 lb. Rated airflows, with static pressure due to 50 ft. of straight duct in each path, are 115 cfm (low speed) and 150 cfm (high speed). Power: 35 W, 90 W. Efficiency: 75% List price: $700.

Optional accessories: Defrost thermostat. Automatic defrost cycle equipment. Motorized fresh-air damper. Remote switches, timing, dehumidistat controls. The complete set of six whole-house models has the following specifications. Note that the second group of three has considerably higher efficiency.

Model	Flowrate (cfm)	Efficiency	Dimensions (in.)	Weight (lb)	Price
210	115-150	75%	46 x 19 x 14	80	About
220	180-240	73%	46 x 19 x 14	80	$700 to
240	325-430	72%	49 x 19 x 18	105	$920
310	110-145	84%	58 x 19 x 14	105	About
320	165-220	84%	58 x 19 x 14	105	$770 to
340	310-415	83%	61 x 19 x 18	130	$1010

Enermatrix, Inc.
PO Box 466, Fargo ND 58107 (701) 232-3330.

Makes two exchangers: EMX 10 and EMX 25.

EMX 10. The core is of crossflow, flat-plate type, and is made of polypropylene. Heat-transfer area: 86 ft^2. The core housing is of enamel coated steel and is insulated with foil-faced urethane foam. There are two drains. Collar diameter: 4 in. The two centrifugal motors are mounted outside the housing. The exhaust blower is larger than the supply blower—to provide higher stale-air outflow than fresh-air inflow, so that frost formation seldom occurs. Against 0.3 in. water static pressure, the blowers provide airflows of 113 cfm (exhaust) and 90 cfm (supply), while using 160 and 85 W of electrical power. There is a filter in the exhaust airstream. Efficiency: 55%. Overall dimensions (core housing and blowers): 28 x 18 x 13 in. Weight: 43 lb. List price: $399.

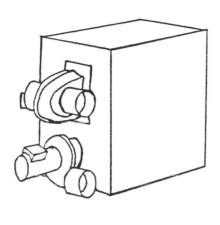

EMX 10

EMX 25. The core is of crossflow, flat-plate type, and is made of polypropylene. Heat-transfer area: 172 ft^2. The core housing is of enamel coated steel and is insulated with foil-faced urethane foam. There are two drains. Dimensions: 39 1/2 x 19 x 14 in. Weight: 50 lb. Diameter of collars: 6 in.

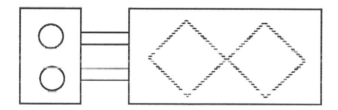

The two centrifugal blowers are mounted in a separate housing, 24 x 16 x 13 in., vibrationally isolated from the core housing. The blowers are equally powerful and against 0.4 in. water static pressure can produce up to 200 cfm flow in each airstream, using up to 150 W of electrical power per blower. The blowers are of variable speed, controlled by a dehumidistat. There is also a defrost control. Weight of blowers and blower housing: 50 lb. Two 10 x 10 in. filters are included. Efficiency: 70%. List price: $899.

Ener-Quip, Inc.
99 E. Kansas St., Hackensack NJ 07601 (201) 487-1015.

Produces EZE-Breathe exchangers. Three models are available: RHR-100, RHR-200, RHR-400. The core of each model is of crossflow type employing aluminum plates. The heat transfer areas of the three models are 100, 200, and 400 ft^2. The housing is of stainless steel and is not insulated. It includes one drain and one filter. There are two axial fans, driven by one motor of variable speed type, controlled manually. Typical efficiency: 65 to 70%. Other characteristics are given in the table below. Options: Defrost control.

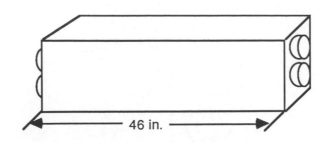

Model	Dimensions (in.)	Weight (lb)	Flowrate (cfm)	Power (W)	Trade Price
RHR 100	46 x 8 x 14	55	50-100	48	$682
RHR 200	46 x 11 x 18	75	100-200	58	$764
RHR 400	46 x 14 x 26	85	200-400	72	$999

Engineering Development, Inc.

4850 North Park Drive, Colorado Springs CO 80907   (303) 599-9080.

Produces two series of Vent-Aire exchangers: ECS-20 (horizontal) and ECS-40 (vertical; new in mid-1986). Each is designed so that a big heating module or cooling module may be attached—so that a single assembly provides ventilation, heat-recovery, heating, cooling.

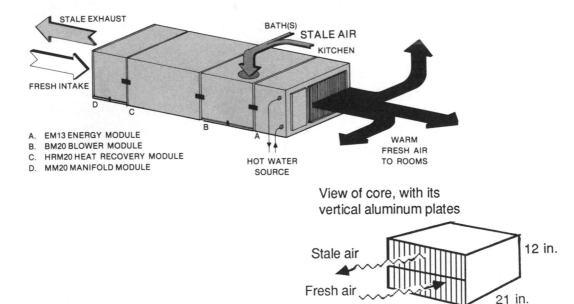

A. EM13 ENERGY MODULE
B. BM20 BLOWER MODULE
C. HRM20 HEAT RECOVERY MODULE
D. MM20 MANIFOLD MODULE

View of core, with its vertical aluminum plates

ECS-20. The core, of counterflow type, employs dimpled aluminum plates providing a heat-transfer area of 180 ft^2. Dimensions: 21 x 19 x 12 in. Weight 25 lb. The housing, of enameled steel, is insulated to R-5.

The manifold module, attached to the cold end of the core module, guides the cold stale air to a duct running to outdoors; also it guides the incoming cold air to the core module. The blower module contains a single motor using 105 W (low speed) or 168 W (high speed). It drives the fresh-air centrifugal blower, producing airflows of 155 and 220 cfm against a static pressure of 0.4 in. water.

Dehumidistat control. There are no filters. Heat-recovery efficiency: about 75 to 80%. Overall dimensions: 13 1/2 x 20 x 51 in. Weight: 68 lb. List price: $806.

Options: 38,000 Btu/hr, 130 lb., electric heat module. Adds $500 to list price. Hydronic heat coil and pump, 130 lb. Adds $500 to list price. Various cooling systems (18,000 to 30,000 Btu/hr). These add $885 to $1185 to the list price. Automatic defrost system. Automatic system for maintaining building pressure balance or specified off-balance.

ECS-4033. The counterflow aluminum core provides a heat transfer area of 172 ft^2. Core dimensions: 21 x 19 x 12 in. Weight: 25 lb. There are two blowers, each using (when at highest speed) 340 W. They are of centrifugal type, and each produces an airflow of up to 300 cfm against a static pressure of 0.4 in. of water. The blower speeds are controllable individually, which permits accurately balancing the airflows or producing a chosen small amount of imbalance. There are two filters. Dehumidistat control. Efficiency: about 70 to 80%.

The heating system, situated within the top of the housing, contains electrical heating elements with an ouput of 37,000 Btu/hr. The housing is a large rectangular *vertical* structure, of galvanized steel, 50 x 28 x 18 in. Overall weight of housing and contents: 122 lb. Collar diameters: 6 in. Big access panel. Drain. List price: $1317.

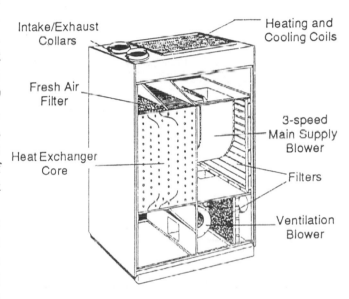

Options: Hydronic heat coil and associated water pump—can be used in place of the electrical heater. Price is same. A variety of air-conditioning (cooling) accessories are available; they deliver cold water to the hydronic coil. Automatic defrost system. Automatic device to maintain airflow balance or a chosen degree of positive or negative imbalance. Timer control for intermittent operation. Various duct-end hoods, screens, etc.

Environment Air Ltd.
PO Box 459, Bouctouche, NB, Canada E0A 1G0   (506) 743-8901.

The company produces a variety of air-to-air heat-exchangers, sometimes called "Enviro Heat-X-Changers," all of which employ heat-pipes. Aluminum fins are bonded to the pipes. The models for use in houses are described in the following table. All have enameled steel housings, all employ, for defrost, fresh-air-intake motor temporary shutdown. All except the smallest models employ blowers of centrifugal type and employ filters of disposable fiberglass.

Typical efficiencies: 60 to 80%. The smallest model, ENV-W60, is designed for wall or window mounting. The other models are for central systems. The company makes also a Model ENV-2000 for use in large buildings. It supplies up to 2300 cfm and has a suggested list price of $5,550 Canadian.

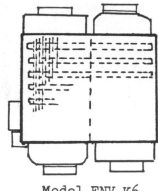

Model ENV-K6

| Model | Dimensions | Weight | Flowrate | Suggsted list price | |
number	(in.)	(lb)	(cfm)	Canadian	US approx.
ENV-W60*	14 x 10 x 7	15	0-27	$530	$382
ENV-135	24.5 x 23.5 x 10	25	0-50	$735	$529
ENV-K6	29 x 27 x 12	60	0-95	$935	$673
ENV-K8	30.5 x 28 x 14	75	0-180	$1,175	$846
ENV-K10	32 x 30 x 16	90	0-255	$1,650	$1,188

* Model ENV-W60 employs axial fans and washable filters.

RB Kanalflakt
1121 Lewis Ave., Sarasota FL 33577 (813) 366-7505.

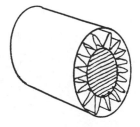

Perspective view of core,
schematic and not to scale.

Markets an exchanger called **Metsovent**, which is produced in Scandinavia and widely sold there but is relatively new to the US. The core, of countercurrent design and made of aluminum, is of cylindrical shape, about 10 in. in diameter and 25 in. long. The heart of the device is a single cylindrical shell that is deeply pleated (accordion folded) so as to provide a heat-transfer area of about 60 ft^2. The central area is blocked off.

The exchanger as a whole includes two motors and two centrifugal blowers that produce 250 cfm airflows against a static pressure of 0.25 in. of water. The efficiency is 60 to 70%. Overall dimensions: 34 x 24 x 21 in. Weight: 67 lb. List price: $595.

Mountain Energy & Resources, Inc.
15800 West Sixth Ave. Golden Co 80401 (303) 279-4971.

The company produces two model of air-to-air heat-exchangers: MER-150 and MER-300.

Mer-150. The core is of heat-pipe, counterflow type. The heat pipes are obtained from QDT, Ltd.

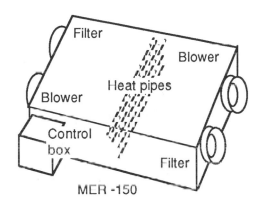

Each heat-pipe consists of an aluminum alloy tube, 5/8 in. diameter and 22 in. long. It has been evacuated, filled with a small amount of refrigerant (freon), and sealed. In operation, the freon is evaporated (boiled) at the warm end of the heat-pipe and condensed at the cool end. The liquid then flows back to the warm end (aided by a wick) and the process repeats.

There are 24 tubes in all. The tubes, mounted strictly horizontally, are press-fit bonded to 130 aluminum fins (in each airstream) 0.07 in. apart. the fins are slightly bent (wavy) for increased stiffness. The fins help carry heat from the warm airstream to the heat-pipes and help carry heat from the heat-pipes to the cool airstream.

The two airstreams are kept fully separated by a vertical partition of galvanized steel.
There are two two-speed, 41-W, electric motors that drive axial-type fans. Each fan, running at high speed and opposed by static pressure of 0.3 in. water, provides an airflow of about 150 cfm. Efficiency: 70%.

The housing, of galvanized steel, is 24 x 24 x 7.5 in. and weighs 67 lb. No insulation is included. If needed, it can be added by the installer. The four collars are 6 in. in diameter. A drain is provided. Removable filters are provided; also a dehumidistat; also automatic freeze protection consisting of a thermostat that turns off the supply fan when frosting threatens. Price: $562.

Options: electric heater for supply duct; stainless steel housing, interval timer, speed control, backdraft damper, duct-end grill.

Model MER-300. Generally similar to the MER-150, except larger (32 x 26 x 13 1/2 in.), heavier (110 lb), employs more heat-pipes (48), produces greater airflow (285 cfm against 0.3 in. water pressure), uses more power (300 W in all). Price: $1150.

NewAire

7009 Raywood Rd., Madison Wi 53713 (608) 221-4499.

Produces three kinds of exchangers: HE-1800C, HE-2500, and HE-4000.

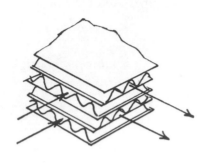

A small portion of the core.

HE-1800C exchanger. Intended for ceiling mounting. The core, of treated paper, is of crossflow type and is made by Mitsubishi in Japan. The core dimensions are 5.75 x 5.75 x 17 in. The heat transfer area is 55 ft^2. The core is removable, for vacuum cleaning—but must not be wetted. The core material is slightly permeable to moisture; thus some moisture is recovered, and within-core condensation occurs very seldom. The two air impellors are driven by a single motor.

Flowrates are said to be 70 cfm against 0.2 in. water static pressure. Power usage: 50 to 60 W. Efficiency: said to be about 70% when the flowrates are 80 cfm. The housing is of galvanized steel. Dimensions: 18 x 17.5 x 13 in. Weight: 45 lb. Two filters are included. No drain is provided, no dehumidistat, no defrost equipment.

The exchanger may be mounted in the ceiling of a bathroom, for example. Stale air from the bathroom enters the exchanges and later flows to the outdoors. Fresh air is ducted from outdoors to the exchanger, and later flows, via a duct, to a ceiling diffuser-grill in an adjacent room. Suggested retail price: $420.

Options: Various humidity and timing controls. A ceiling light of fluorescent type. Deluxe silver or gold diffuser.

HE-2500 exchanger. Core: generally similar to that of the HE-1800 exchanger: crossflow; treated paper. Core dimensions: 12 x 12 x 10 in. Heat-transfer area: 140 ft^2. The two centrifugal blowers produce, against 0.3 in. water static pressure, flowrates of 100 cfm, using (together) 160 W. Efficiency said to be "up to 78%." Single speed, manual-control operation. The housing is of painted galvaneel. Dimensions 30 x 20 x 12 in. Weight: 50 lb. Insulation: one inch of foil-faced fiberglass. two washable permanent filters are included. Collar diameter: 6 in. No drain pan or defrost system. Suggested retail price: $535.

Options: 24-hr timer control, polyethylene core, drain pan, condensate fitting, defrost control. Prices with options: $595 to $695.

HE-4000 exchanger. Generally similar to HE-2500 except larger (31 x 21 x 20 in.), heavier (75 lb.), and more powerful. Each blower provides, at 0.36 in. water static pressure, 150 cfm. Total power: 240 W. Collar diameter: 8 in. Efficiency claimed: "up to 78%." No drain pan or defrost system. Suggested retail price: $717. Options: Same as for HE-2500.

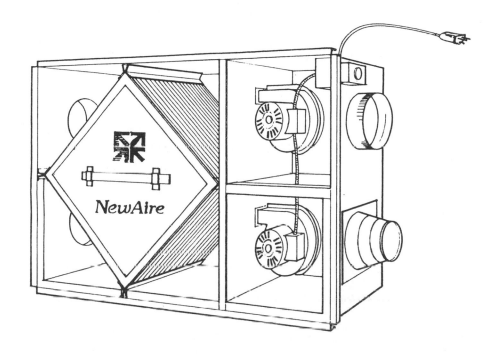

Nutech Energy Systems Inc.

124 Newbold Court, London, Ontario, Canada R3E 1P6 (204) 774-2223.

Makes four kinds of crossflow exchangers, called **Lifebreath** exchangers: 100 Standard, 200 MAX, 200 Standard, and 300 DCS. All four kinds are of crossflow type, employing dimpled aluminum plates. The housings are of steel. There are two blowers and two removable washable filters.

A dehumidistat is included, and automatic defrost is provided. Collar diameters range from 5 in. to 7 in.

In Models **200 MAX** and **300 DCS**, defrosting is accomplished by a microprocessor-controlled damper in the fresh-air stream. In Model 200 STD it is accomplished by automatic 2.5-min stopping of the fresh-air blower and use of electrical heat.

Model	Dimensions (in.)	Wgt. (lb.)	Flowrate* (cfm)	Total power (W)	Efficiency	Typical price retail US
100 Std.	24x10.5x18.5	40	60	40	60-70%	About $570
200 Max	31x15x19	70	175	70	75%	About $800
200 Std.	As above except uses electrical heat defrost system					
300 DCS	49x15x19	100	210	150	77%	About $1000

*Flowrate in each airstream, against 0.4 in. water static pressure.

QDT, Ltd.

1000 Singleton Blvd., Dallas TX 75212-5214   (214) 741-1993. (Before June 1987 the address was 701 N. First St., Garland, TX 75040 and the company name was Q-Dot Corp.)
The company produces two models of "Safe Air Exchangers" (SAE): SAE-150 and SAE-250.

Model SAE-150. The core is of heat-pipe, counterflow type. Each heat-pipe consists of an aluminum alloy tube, 5/8 in. diameter, evacuated, sealed, and filled with a small amount of refrigerant (freon). This is vaporized at the warm end of the tube and condensed at the cool end. There are 48 tubes in all. The tubes, oriented horizontal, are bonded to 75 aluminum fins that are spaced 1/7 inch apart on centers.

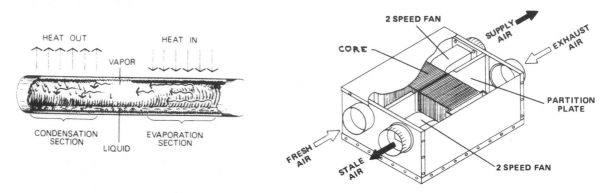

The fins are slightly corrugated for increased heat transfer. The fins help carry heat from the warm airstream to the heat-pipes and help carry heat from the heat-pipes to the cool airstream. The two airstreams are kept fully separated by a vertical partition of galvanized steel.

There are two blowers, each driven by a 118 W electric two-speed motor. Total power usage: 236 W. Each blower, running at high speed and subject to the static pressure from 40 ft. of 6-in.-diameter duct with one 90-deg. turn, produces a flowrate of 150 cfm. Efficiency: 70%.

The housing, of special 20-gauge galvanized steel, is 28 1/2 x 22 x 12 1/2 in. and weighs 94 lb. It is internally insulated with 1/2 inch of NPFA 90 black mat insulation. Each of the four collars is 6 in. diameter. There is one regular drain and one overflow drain. A defrost cycle is included. List price: $599. Options include filter, humidistat, timer, electric heater, two-speed blower switch.

Model SAE-250. This model is similar except larger (32 x 28 x 14 in., heavier (124 lb), and produces a greater airflow (250 cfm in each airstream). Total power usage: 350 W.
List price: $716.

Raydot Inc.

145 Jackson Ave., Cokato MN 55321   (612) 286-2103.

The Raydot exchanger for houses has a long, slender core of counterflow type. It employs no large set of closely spaced plates, but rather employs three long chambers: a central one for stale air and two long ones (above and below) for fresh air. In cross section the separator sheets, or septums, are deeply formed in a double V manner, to increase heat-transfer area. Although the overall width of a chamber is only 12 in., the effective width is about 16 in. At regular intervals along the chambers there are foam blocks, likewise having double V cross section, that cause the airflow to be turbulent, to increase the heat transfer.

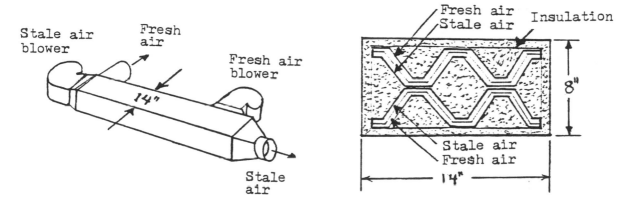

The effective length is about 96 in. The heat-transfer area is about 2 x 16 x 96 = 3,072 in.^{2} or about 21 ft^2. Each of the four faces of the housing is insulated with one inch of urethane foam. A drain is provided. There are two variable-speed, manually controlled, 0.08 hp blowers which produce, under typical static pressures, about 75 cfm at low speed and about 220 cfm at high speed. The respective efficiencies claimed are 82% and 74%. There are no filters and there is no defrost system. Retail price: $890. Options: dehumidistat, filters, duct accessories.

Standex Energy Systems

1090 Legion Rd., PO Box 1168, Detroit Lakes MN 56501 (218) 847 9258.
Makes two kinds of "May-Aire" air-to-air heat-exchangers: MA-110 and MA-240.

MA-110. The core, of 0.007-inch thick corrugated aluminum plates, is of crossflow type. The housing, of brushed aluminum, is 17.5 x 17.5 x 7.5 in. It includes four 5-in.-diameter ports. Removable washable filters are mounted at two ports, and 17 W variable-speed axial fans are mounted at the other two ports, producing up to 110 cfm with no external static pressure and 60 cfm with 0.2 in. static pressure. Overall maximum power usage: 34 W. Efficiency: Up to 80%. Overall weight: 27 lb. A drain is included.

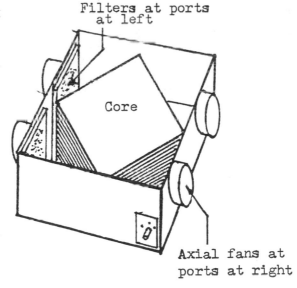

The defrost system involves briefly turning off the fresh air fan whenever the fresh air delivered to the room is colder than 32°F. The fan is turned on again when the temperature rises to 55°F. Price: $550.

MA-240. This is generally similar except that the housing is larger (22 x 23 x 8.5 in.), the fans are more powerful (32 W each) and deliver a greater airflow (240 cfm against no static pressure and

180 cfm against 0.2 in. static pressure). Power consumption is greater: up to 64 W. Efficiency: 73%. Overall weight: 45 lb. Port diameters: 6 in. Suggested list price: $596.

Star Heat Exchanger Corp.

B109-1772 Broadway St., Port Coquitlam, B. C., Canada V3C 2M8   (604) 942-0525.
The company makes three large models (165, 200, and 300) and one small model (Nova).

Large models: Model 165, Model 200, Model 300. These provide airflows of 165, 200, and 300 cfm respectively when there is no opposing static pressure, and provide about 160, 170, and 280 cfm against a static pressure of 0.15 in. water. (This low value of static pressure is used because the manufacturer has adopted the practice of using ducts of especially large diameter: 6, 7, and 8 in.) The claimed efficiency values, with the 160, 170, and 280 cfm flowrates and with ambient temperatures of 30 to 50°F, are in the range 60 to 80%. Power consumptions have the nominal values of 66, 66, and 132 W.

A key feature of the exchangers is the "interfaced tube type core." This consists of a large array of compactly arranged plastic tubes each of which has a rectangular (5 x 5 mm) cross section. The unique feature of the core is that each tube that carries stale air is totally flanked by (four) tubes that carry fresh air, and each tube that carries fresh air is totally flanked by (four) tubes that carry stale air. Thus, an exceptionally large heat-transfer area is provided without significant penalty on pneumatic resistance. To accommodate this new type of core design, an entirely new plastic extrusion method was needed, and also a special manifold arrangement.

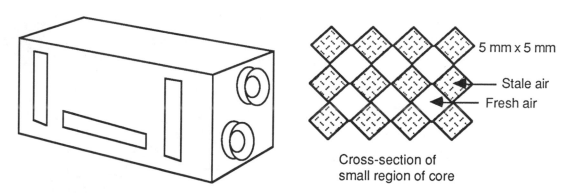

Cross-section of
small region of core

A computerized monitor and control system balances the two flows every 5 seconds and provides a continuous LED display of flowrates. The three models have the overall dimensions 12.5 x 40 x 15 in., 25 x 39 x 15 in., and 25 x 39 x 15 in. respectively. The weights are 22, 40, and 44 lb. All of the models employ counterflow airstreams; axial, sealed, ball-bearing fans; variable speed control; automatic defrost; high-efficiency disposable pleated filters in both airstreams; drain for condensate; plastic ABS case. The warranty period is 5 years. The typical retail prices are about US $642, $817, and $998 respectively.

Nova exchanger. This is a small counterflow plate-type exchanger with dimensions 25 x 16 x 7.5 in. Weight: 12 lb. Airflow under no external static pressure: 70 cfm. Nominal power rating: 34 W. The typical retail price is about $359.

XchangeAIR Corp.

7th and University Drive North, PO Box 1565, Fargo ND 58107 (701) 237-0491.
Provides three models: BDR-95, BDR-210, and BDR-315.

Model BDR-95. The core, of plastic (Coroplast), is of crossflow type. The housing is of 24-gauge galvanized steel, painted. The four collars have a diameter of 4 in. Insulation: 3/4 inch of urethane foam. The two centrifugal blowers are mounted externally on the vertical front face of the housing. Each provides, under 0.3 in. of water static pressure, an airflow of 80 cfm.

Total power usage: 122 W. Efficiency: 73 to 79%. Overall dimensions, including the external blowers: height 15 in., width 21 in., depth 21 in. Weight: 40 lb. A defrost control and a dehumidistat are included. No speed control is included, and the equipment must be wired during installation. Price: $540.

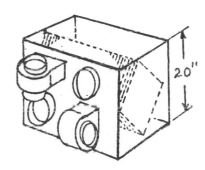

Model BDR-210. This is much the same except larger (20 x 22 x 28 in.), heavier (70 lb), employs more powerful blowers (up to 250 W) providing greater airflow (135 cfm). Collar diameter: 6 in. A variable speed control is provided, as well as a dehumidistat and a defrost system employing a temperature sensor that temporarily turns off the fresh-air blower when frosting threatens. Suggested list price: $740.

Model BDR-315. Like Model BDR-210 except larger (24 x 31 x 34 in.), heavier (100 lb), and provides greater airflow (255 cfm). Collar diameter: 8 in. Suggested list price: $975.

XeteX Inc.

3600 E. 28 St., Minneapolis MN 55406 (612) 724-3101.
(This company took over, a few years ago, from Heat-X-Changer Co. and from EER Products, Inc.) Produces six models: HX-50, HX-100, HX-150, HX-200, HX-250, HX-350.

Model	Dimensions (in.)	Weight (lb)	Flowrate* (cfm)	Power total (W)	Heat transfer area (sq ft)	List price
HX-50	19 x 11.5 x 7	25	51	73	31	$395
HX-100	24.5 x 11.5 x 12	40	85	122	104	$676
HX-150	24 x 18 x 12.5	50	119	160	167	$788
HX-200	24 x 25.5 x 13	60	182	240	250	$902
HX-250	32 x 18 x 22	75	300	250	512	$1242
HX-350	40 x 25.5 x 22	125	410	314	766	$1533

*Flowrate in each airstream, against 0.4 in. water static pressure.

Model HX-50. Somewhat similar to Model HX-100 described below, but smaller. Airflow against 0.4 in. water static pressure is 51 cfm. Employs a single motor. 73 W power usage. Efficiency: 62%. Dimensions: 19 x 11.5 x 7 in. List price: $395.

Model HX-100 Core, employing aluminum plates, is of crossflow type. Each of the two 61 W blowers produces airflows of 85 cfm against a static pressure of 0.4 in. water. Efficiency: 80%. Housing, of galvanized steel, includes 1 in. of foil-faced fiberglass insulation, drain pan, defrost control, and 4-in. collars. List price: $676. Options: intake filter, backdraft damper, intake and exhaust hoods.

Models HX-150, HX-200, HX-250, HX-350. These are generally similar but larger. See table below. Efficiency: 80%. Collar diameters range from 4 in. to 8 in.

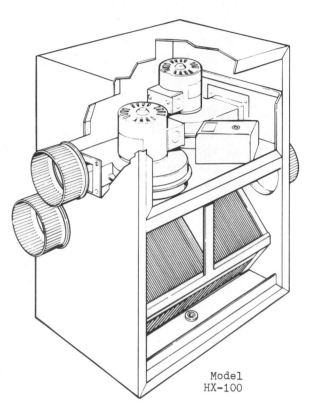

Model
HX-100

EXCHANGERS MANUFACTURED OVERSEAS

The exchangers distributed by American Aldes Ventilation Corp, discussed on a previous page, are made in France.

Bahco (AB) Ventilation, of Sweden, makes an advanced exchanger called Minimaster designed to be installed in the hood above a cooking stove. Information may be obtained from Karlson Home Central Inc., 2605 Broadway Ave., Evanston IL 60201.

Flakt Company, of West Germany, makes a crossflow-type exchanger called Rexovent. Information may be obtained from Semco Manufacturing Inc., PO Box 1797, Columbia MO 65205. Semco produces large rotary exchangers for use in hospitals, hotels, industrial plants, etc.

Reclaire Ltd., of England, markets an Indola R2000 crossflow-type exchanger through its subsidiary, Colchester Fan Marketing Co. Ltd., Hillbottom Rd., Sands Industrial Estate, Highwycombe, Bucks, HP12 4HR, England.

Temovex AB, of Sweden, makes a counterflow-type exchanger, called Model 480, that can be installed horizontally or vertically and can be supplied with or without an electrostatic dust precipitator. Address: Box 111, S 265 01, Astorp, Sweden.

AIR-TO-AIR HEAT EXCHANGER SPECIFICATIONS SUMMARY

This summary shows, for nearly every major manufacturer, product name, overall dimensions, weight, flowrate, efficiency, blower power, and price in US dollars. All subject to change. In some instances important controls and accessories are not included in standard models. Also, stated flowrates depend strongly on assumptions as to static pressure head. Efficiency values depend strongly on flowrates chosen. Most of the stated prices are list prices; actual prices may be lower. Often dealers may buy at discount prices. Some performance figures have not been independently verified and may be overstated.

ACS-Hoval
    PC-130   47 x 17.5 x 12 in.   46 lb   110-160 cfm   240 W   52-65% $635.
    PC-230 66.5 x 17.5 x 12 in.   66 lb   215-285 cfm   426 W   68-85% $1,005.
    Also other models.

Air Changer Marketing
    Exchanger components. Copolymer cores: CC6 and CC6S.
    Fan and control assemblies DRAP-150 and DRAP-275.

AirXchange, Inc.
    Model 502CA   29 x 17.5 x 10 in.   44 lb   150-200 cfm   150 W   Up to 80% $619.
    Model 570   23 x 14 x 11 in.   25 lb   70 cfm   50 W   Up to 80% $498.
    Also other models.

American Aldes Ventilation Corp
    VMP-H Core assembly is 38.5 x 20 x 11.5 in. 22 lb. Efficiency at 90 cfm: 70%. Blower system, 16 x 15 x 12 in., is separate. Flowrates are 85 to 160 cfm. 100-200 W. Price: $1000. Price with many accessories: $1500. Unique options: VMP-K self-regulating inlet port and Hygro humidity-controlled outlet port.

Aston Industries Inc.
    Separate components. Thermatube 2300 with glass-tube core and filter. Two blowers. $500 to $600.

Berner International Corp.
    EM-120   21.5 x 12.5 x 8 in.   21 lb   30-55 cfm   25-40 W   75-82% $390.
    EM-250   31 x 28 x 14 in.   73 lb   70-120 cfm   70-75%   About $1000.
    EM-500   40 x 28 x 14 in.   106 lb   170-300 cfm   90-260 W   71-80%   About $1400.
    All three models employ desiccant-coated rotors.

Blackhawk Industries Inc.
    In mid-1987 were preparing a new line of sophisticated exchangers.

139

Bossaire
  BX-75   24.5 x 11.5 x 12 in.   40 lb   75 cfm   120 W $660.
  BX-350   40 x 25.5 x 22 in.   125 lb   350 cfm   310 W $1,500.
  Also four models of intermediate size.

Conservation Energy Systems Inc.
  VanEE 1000 Basic 25 x 21 x 13 in.   65 lb   100 cfm   70% $445.
  VanEE 1000 LD   Similar but includes variable speed drive and Frostbuster. $577.
  VanEE 2000 SLD   34 x 21 x 17 in.   75 lb   220-256 cfm   60-76%.
  Variable speed drive and Frostbuster.
  VanEE 7000   Similar but larger.   47 x 20 x 19 in.   Up to 700 cfm $1650.

Des Champs Laboratories Inc.
  Single-room model EZV-175A 22 x 16.5 x 9 in.   30 lb   75 cfm   75% $310-$340.
  Whole-house model EZV-210 46 x 18 x 14 in.   80 lb   150 cfm   90 W   75% $700.
  Whole-house model EZV-340   61x19x18 in.   130 lb   310-415 cfm   83% $1010.
  Also other models.

Enermatrix, Inc.
  EMX-10   28 x 18 x 13 in.   43 lb   90-113 cfm   80-160 W   55% $399.
  EMX-25   39.5 x 19 x 14 in.   50 lb   200 cfm   150 W   70% $899.

Ener-Quip, Inc.
  EZE-Breathe RHR-100 46 x 8 x 14 in.   55 lb   50-100 cfm   48 W   65-70% $682.
  EZE-Breathe RHR-200 46 x 11 x 18 in.   75 lb   100-200 cfm   58 W   65-70% $764.
  EZE-Breathe RHR-400 46 x 14 x 26 in.   85 lb   200-400 cfm   72 W   65-70% $999.

Engineering Development, Inc.
  Vent-Aire ECS-20   21 x 19 x 12 in.   25 lb   155-220 cfm   105-168 W   75-80% $806.
  Vent-Aire ECS-4033 50 x 28 x 18 in.   122 lb   220 cfm   340 W   70-80% $1,317.

Environment Air Ltd.
  Enviro-Heat-X-Changer ENV-W60   14 x 10 x 7 in.   15 lb   27 cfm   60-80% $382.
  Enviro-Heat-X-Changer ENV-K10   32 x 30 x 16 in.   90 lb   255 cfm   60-80% $1,188.

Kanalflakt (RB)
  Metsovent exchanger 10 in. diam. x 25 in. long 62 lb 250 cfm 60-70% $595.

Mountain Energy & Resources, Inc.
  MER-150   24 x 24 x 7.5 in.   67 lb   150 cfm   41 W   70% $562.
  MER-300   32 x 26 x 13.5 in.   110 lb   285 cfm   300 W   70% $1,150.

NewAire

HE-1800	18 x 17.5 x 13 in.	45 lb	80 cfm	80 W		70%	$420.
HE-2500	30 x 20 x 12 in.	50 lb	100 cfm	320 W	Up to 78%		$535.
HE-4000	31 x 21 x2 0 in.	75 lb	150 cfm	480 W	Up to 78%		$717.

Nutech Energy Systems Inc.

100 Std.	24 x 10.5 x 18.5 in.	40 lb	60 cfm	40 W		$570.
200 MAX	31 x 15 x 19 in.	70 lb	175 cfm	70 W	75%	$800.
300 DCS	49 x 15 x 19 in.	100 lb	210 cfm	150 W	77%	$1,000.

QDT, Ltd.

Safe Air Exchanger SAE-150	28.5 x 22 x 12.5 in.	95 lb	150 cfm	236 W	70%	$599.
Safe Air Exchanger SAE-250	32 x 28 x 14 in.	124 lb	250 cfm	350 W	70%	$716.

Raydot Inc.

Raydot exchanger. Overall dimensions, incl. blowers: 126 x 34 x 8 in. 75 cfm 82% $890.

Standex Energy Systems

MA-110	17.5 x 17.5 x 7.5 in.	27 lb	60 cfm	34 W	Up to 80%	$550.
MA-240	22 x 23 x 8.5 in.	45 lb	180 cfm	64 W	73%	$596.

Star Heat Exchanger Corp.

Model 165	12.5 x 40 x 15 in.	22 lb	160 cfm	66 W	60-80%	$642.
Model 200	25 x 39 x 15 in.	40 lb	170 cfm	66 W	60-80%	$817.
Model 300	25 x 39 x 15 in.	44 lb	280 cfm	132 W	60-80%	$998.
Nova	25 x 16 x 7.5 in.	12 lb	70 cfm	34 W		$359.

XchangeAIR Corp.

BDR-95	15 x 21 x 21 in.	40 lb	80 cfm	122 W	73-79%	$540.
BDR-210	20 x 22 x 28 in.	70 lb	135 cfm	250 W	73-79%	$740.
BDR-315	24 x 31 x 34 in.	100 lb	255 cfm	250 W	73-79%	$975.

Xetex Inc.

HX-50	19 x 11.5 x 7 in.	25 lb	51 cfm	73 W	62%	$395.
HX-150	24 x 18 x 12.5 in.	50 lb	119 cfm	160 W	79%	$788.
HX-350	40 x 25.5 x 22 in.	125 lb	410 cfm	314 W	80%	$1,533.

Also other models.

INDEX OF TRADE NAMES

Trade Name	Manufacturer
AE-70, AE-200	AirXchange Inc.
Air Changer	Air Changer Marketing
Aldes	American Aldes Ventilation Corp.
Atic 2000	Aston Industries Inc.
BDR	XchangeAIR Corp.
BX	Bossaire
CC6	Air Changer Marketing
DRAP	Air Changer Marketing
ECS-20	Engineering Development, Inc.
EM-120, EM-500	Berner International Corp.
EMX-10, EMX-25	Enermatrix, Inc.
ENV	Environmental Air Ltd.
Enviro	Environmental Air Ltd.
EZE-Breathe	Ener-Quip, Inc.
EZV	Des Champs Laboratories Inc.
E-Z-Vent	Des Champs Laboratories Inc.
HE	NewAire
Heat-X-Changer	XeteX Inc.
Hygro	American Aldes Ventilation Corp.
HX	XeteX Inc.
Indola R2000	Reclaire Ltd.
K6, K8, K10	Environmental Air Ltd.
Lifebreath	Nutech Energy Systems Inc.
MA-110, MA-240	Standex Energy Systems Inc.
May-Aire	Standex Energy Systems Inc.
MER-150, MER-300	Mountain Energy & Resources, Inc.
Metsovent	RB Kanalflakt
Minimaster	Bahco (AB) Ventilation
Nova	Star Heat Exchanger Corp.
PB, PC	ACS-Hoval
Q-Dot	QDT, Ltd.
Raydot	Raydot Inc.
Rexovent	Flakt Company
RHR	Ener-Quip, Inc.
SAE-150, SAE-250	QDT, Ltd.
Thermatube 2300	Aston Industries Inc.
VanEE	Conservation Energy Systems, Inc.
Vent-Aire	Engineering Development, Inc.
VMP-H, HVP-K	American Aldes Ventilation Corp.
100 Std., 200 MAX, 300 DCS	Nutech Energy Systems Inc.

Chapter 20
Economics of Exchanger Use

Here a very simple subject is discussed: how much money does a homeowner save by employing an air-to-air heat exchanger to freshen the air in his house—compared to merely using forced ventiliation with *no* recovery of heat from the outgoing air?

The answer is: a great deal, if the house is in a cold climate and a high rate of fresh-air input (such as 200 cfm) is desired. Under such circumstances an air-to-air heat exchanger "pays for itself" in about three to seven years.

SAVING DURING FIRST YEAR

It is self-evident that if, throughout the first year of use of a certain heat-exchanger (which has a sensible-heat-recovery efficiency of 75%), this exchanger supplies 200 ft^3 of fresh air each minute to a house in a 5000 °F degree-day location, the amount of heat recovered is

$$(200 \text{ ft}^3/\text{min}) (60 \text{ min/hr}) (24 \text{ hr/day}) (0.074 \text{ lb/ft}^3) (0.24 \text{ Btu lb } °F) (5000 °F \text{ DD}) (75\%)$$
$$= 19.2 \text{ million Btu per winter.}$$

If the same amount of fresh air had been supplied with no heat recovery, and if a 70% efficient oil furnace (using oil at $1.20/gal.) had been used to heat this air to 65°F (i.e., with a cost of $12 per million Btu), the expenditure would have been 19.2 x $12 = $230.

Thus the overall saving, per winter, from use of the exchanger is $230 minus the cost of electric power used by the exchanger blower motors—about $40 to $80, depending on the exchanger and on the local price of electricity.

Choice Of Degree-Day Figure

Air-to-air heat exchangers are especially useful in tightly built houses. Usually, such houses are well insulated and may require little or no auxiliary heat as long as the outdoor temperature exceeds 55°F say (or even lower temperature for houses that are especially well insulated and receive much heat from light bulbs, cooking stoves, etc., and from solar radiation). In other words, the heat saved by an air-to-air heat exchanger when the outdoor temperature exceeds 55°F, say, is not needed at that time, in such a house, and so has little or no monetary value. In estimating the dollar saving by the exchanger, one should use degree-day values based—not on 65°F—but on 55°F or whatever temperature is appropriate.

Overall Cost of Exchanger

A person considering buying an exchanger should consider not only the F.O.B. purchase cost but also (1) the cost of shipping and installing the exchanger, (2) the annual operating cost (cost of electrical power), usually about 1/10 or 1/5 of the saving and thus nearly negligible, and (3) the annual maintenance cost, which is negligible ordinarily.

Saving Relative To Use Of Gas Or Electricity

Relative to the use of a 70% efficient gas furnace with gas priced at $4 per 1000 ft^3 or $5.7 per million Btu, the saving (in the above-stated example) would be about $113, i.e., about half as great. Relative to the use of electricity at 7¢/kWh, or $20.6 per million Btu, the saving would be about twice as great as with oil, i.e., about $400.

GENERAL FORMULA FOR SAVING DURING FIRST YEAR

The general formula is: Dollar saving during the first winter (from use of the given exhanger with given sensible-heat-recovery efficiency) is the product ABCDEF where:

   A = (rate of fresh air input, in ft^3/min)(60 min/hr)(24 hr/day)
   B = 0.074 lb/ft^3
   C = 0.24 Btu/(lb ^{o}F)
   D = degree day value
   E = efficiency of sensible-heat recovery
   F = cost of auxiliary heat in dollars per Btu.

Combining all of the above-listed constants into a single constant, the formula boils down to this:

   $ saving 1st yr = (25.6 Btu min/°F day ft^3) (rate of air input, ft^3 min.) (DD) (Efficiency)
                                         (Dollars/Btu)

or, very briefly: Saving = (25.6) (cfm) (DD) (Efficiency) ($/Btu).

COST SAVINGS

If the cost of auxiliary heat escalates at 15% per year, then the saving during the first five years of use of an exchanger is about 35% more than would be the case if there were no escalation. Using, as first-year costs of auxiliary heat, the figures given above (namely $12, $5.7, and $20.6 per million Btu using oil, gas, and electricity), the five year saving with 15% escalation, for the specific case discussed on the previous page, is $1550, $750, and $2670 respectively.

The ten-yer saving, again assuming 15% escalation in cost of auxiliary heat, one finds the saving to be about $4670, $2220, and $8030 respectively.

These are big numbers! Several times the cost of the exchanger!

SOME POSSIBLE OTHER BONUSES

If the exchanger provides transfer of heat only, the house occupant may enjoy there bonuses:

In winter, the load on the furnace is reduced and accordingly a smaller cheaper furnace may suffice. Or perhaps the furnace may be dispensed with entirely; perhaps a small electrical heater can provide all the auxiliary heat needed.

In summer, the load on the air conditioning system is reduced. A smaller cheaper conditioner may suffice. Possibly the occupants can get by with no conditioner.

If the exchanger transfers both heat and water, humidification needs in winter are reduced and dehumidification needs in summer are reduced.

Federal and state governments may provide certain tax benefits to persons who install heat-exchangers.

Added Note

An excellent treatment of the cost-effectiveness of air-to-air heat exchangers may be found in *Energy Sourcebook* (Bibliography item M-97), pages 592-597, and in a report by G. D. Roseme et al of Lawrence Berkeley Laboratory, Univ. of Calif. (Bibliography item U-520-13).

BUYING AN EXCHANGER

Before buying an air-to air heat-exchanger, the householder should address these questions:

What kinds of pollutants are present in my house? Are they sufficiently concentrated to be health hazards or to produce discomfort? What are their sources? Can they be eliminated?

Do I really need an exchanger? Or is my house leaky enough so that, nearly always, natural infiltration provides all the fresh air needed? If not, can I get by merely by opening a window ?

If I buy an exchanger, am I doing so primarily to supply fresh air, or primarily to avoid excessive humidity?

Is the recovery of latent heat (from moist indoor air) a major goal?

Do I intend to use the exchanger in summer also?

Is a fresh air supply needed in just one room? Or in several rooms? If the latter, will I feel obliged to install a duct system that will serve several rooms? Would it be better to buy several small exchangers and put one in each room—and avoid the need for ducts?

What capacity is needed? Will 60 to 100 cfm suffice? Or is a higher capacity needed?

Is the climate cold enough that frost formation and clogging of passages in the exchanger could be serious threats?

How elaborate a control system is wanted? Is a versatile and automatic system necessary? Or will manual controls suffice?

Where, exactly, would the exchanger be installed? Will there be adequate access for installing it and, subsequently, inspecting and servicing it?

Who will install it and who will take the overall responsibility for seeing that it performs properly?

What price is acceptable? What annual operating cost is acceptable?

Will the exchanger be truly cost-effective?

Having considered these questions, the householder should decide what type of exchanger he wants: rotary, or fixed with laminar flow, or fixed with turbulent flow. Also he should decide which specific make and model is most appropriate, whether a suitable dealer is near enough at hand, whether price, delivery period, and warranty are satisfactory.

Of course, the householder would do well to consult with available friends and experts who have had experience with exchangers.

Appendix 1
Units and Conversions

Energy	1 J	= exactly 1 newton-meter
		i.e., 10^5 dyne-meter
		i.e., 10^7 erg
		i.e., 1 watt-second
		= 2.778 x 10^{-7} kWh
		= 9.478 x 10^{-4} Btu
	1 kWh	= exactly (3600)(1000) watt-second
		i.e., 3.6 x 10^6 J
		i.e., 3.6 x 10^{13} erg
		= 3.412 x 10^3 Btu
	1 Btu	= exactly 1 (lb. H_2O at 63°F)(°F)
		= 1.055 x 10^3 J
		= 1.055 x 10^{10} erg
		= 2.931 x 10^{-4} kWh
		= 778.2 ft lb.
	1 therm	= exactly 10^5 Btu

1 42-gal. barrel of oil = 5.8 x 10^6 Btu

1 cubic foot of natural gas = 1031 Btu

1 lb. coal = 1.25 x 10^4 Btu

Length	1 ft.	= 0.305 m
Area	1 ft^2	= 0.0929 m^2
Volume	1 ft^3	= 0.0283 m^3
Mass	1 lb.	= 0.4536 kg
Force	1 lb force	= 4.448 N

Pressure
1 pound force/in^2 = 6.9 kN/m^2 = 6.9 kPa
1 atm. = 14.7 pound force/in^2 = 101.3 kPa = 407 in. H_2O

Viscosity
(i.e., absolute viscosity, dynamic viscosity)
1 poise = 1 P = 1 gram/(sec. cm.) = 100 centipoise
1 pound force, sec./ft^2 = 0.047 Pa sec.
Viscosity in centipoise x 0.000,672 = viscosity in lb/(sec. ft.)
Viscosity in centipoise x 0.000,020,9 = viscosity in (lb. force)(sec./$ft.^2$)
Example for air at 70°F and atm. pressure: viscosity is
0.018 centipoise, or 0.000,000,375 (lb. force x sec.)/($ft.^2$),
or 0.000012 lb. mass/(sec. ft.)

Heat flowrate	1 Btu/hr	= 0.293 W
Thermal conductivity	1 Btu/(ft hr °F)	= 1.730 W/(m °C)
Coefficient of heat transfer	1 Btu/(ft^2 hr °F)	= 5.678 W/(m^2 °C)
Specific heat capacity	1 Btu/(lb. °F)	= 4.186 x 10^3 J/(kg °C)
Enthalpy	1 Btu/lb.	= 2.326 J/g

Appendix 2
Sources of Information

American Council for an Energy-Efficient Economy, 1001 Connecticut Ave., NW, Suite 535, Washington DC 20036.

American Society of Heating Ventilating and Air Conditioning Engineers (ASHRAE), 1791 Tullie Circle, Atlanta GA 30329. Has issued many standards and guidelines, including Standard 90.2 on Energy Efficient New Residential Construction.

American Solar Energy Association, 2030 17th St., Boulder CO 80302.

Building Thermal Envelope Co-ordinating Council, 101 15th St. NW, Suite 700, Washington DC 20005.

Canada Mortage and Housing Corporation, 682 Montreal Rd., Ottawa, Canada K1A 0P7.

Canadian Home Builder's Association, 331 Cooper St., Ottawa, Canada K2P 0G5.

Canadian Standards Association, 178 Rexdale Blvd., Rexdale, Ontario, Canada M9W 1K3.

Corbet, Hanson, and Associates, Box 3838, Butte MT 59702. Sells detailed plans of carefully designed superinsulated houses.

Energy Efficient Building Association, PO Box 1115, Pine Island MN 55963.

Energy, Mines and Resources Canada, Building Energy Technology Transfer Program (BETT), 580 Booth St., Ottawa, Canada K1A 0E4. Distributes a wide variety of reports and booklets on energy efficient buildings.

Heating, Refrigeration and Air Conditioning Institute, 5468 Dundas St. West, Suite 226, Islington, Ontario, Canada M9B 6E3.

Home Ventilating Institute, 30 West University Drive, Arlington Heights IL 60004.

International Intelligent Building Association, 1815 H St. NW, Suite 100, Washington DC 20006.

National Association of Home Builders, Technical Service Department, 15th and M Streets NW, Washington DC 20002. The NAHB operates a National Research Center and has issued Thermal Performance Guidelines.

National Bureau of Standards, Center for Building Technology, Gaithersburg MD 20234. Issues reports on basic technologies used in constructing superinsulated houses.

National Center for Appropriate Technology, Box 3838, Butte MT 59702. Distributes miscellaneous information on superinsulation and also detailed plans.

National Research Council of Canada, Division of Building Research, Saskatoon, Saskatchewan, Canada S7N 0W9. Was, but no longer is, one of the most active groups in developing and publicizing superinsulation.

Ontario Research Foundation, Sheridan Park, Missisauga, Ontario, Canada L5K 1B3. Operates a test facility.

Solar Energy Research Institute (SERI), 1617 Cole Blvd., Golden CO 80401.

Thermal Insulation Manufacturers Association, 7 Kirby Lane, Mt. Kisco NY 10549.

University of Illinois, Small Homes Council and Building Research Council, 1 East St. Mary's Road, Champaign IL 61820. Produces a great variety of pamphlets and booklets on energy-efficient house construction.

Bibliography

BOOKS

A-52 Alberta Agriculture, *Low Energy Home Designs*. 1982. 94 pp. Free. Alberta Department of Agriculture, Home and Community Design Branch, Room 401, 10508 82nd Ave., Edmonton, Alberta, Canada T6E 2A4. Detailed plans of 20 kinds of superinsulated houses.

A-54 Alberta Agriculture, *New House Planning and Idea Book*. 1983. $8.95. Brick House Publishing Co., PO Box 512, 3 Main St., Andover MA 01810. Many detailed plans. Contents somewhat similar to those of above-mentioned book.

B-330 Blomsterberg, A. K., and D. T. Harrje, "Approaches to Evaluation of Air Infiltration Energy Losses in Buildings," *ASHRAE Transactions,* Vol. 85, 1979. Part 1.

B-417 Booth, Don, *Sun-Earth Buffering and Superinsulation*. 1983. 230 pp. Paperback. $17.95. Community Builders, Shaker Rd., Canterbury NH 03224. Detailed information, based on much practical experience, on a variety of low-cost energy-conserving houses employing superinsulation and some passive solar heating.

C-702 Cook, Jeffrey, *Award-Winning Passive Solar House Designs*. 1984. 175 pp. $11. Garden Way Publishing Co., Pownal, VT 05261. Some of the houses described qualify as superinsulated.

D-11 Dallaire, Gene, "Zero Energy House: Bold, Low-Cost Breakthrough That May Revolutionize Housing," *Civil Engineering* (May 1980), 47-59.

E-440 Energy, Mines and Resources Canada: Building Energy Technology Transfer Program (BETT), *Energy Conservation and House Basements*. BETT Publication No. 82.01. 1982. 144 pp. 580 Booth St., Ottawa, Canada K1A 0E4. Detailed instructions concerning walls, sills, basements, and vapor barriers.

E-446 _____. *Air-Vapour Barriers*. BETT Publication No. 84-2406/2. Distributed by Canadian Home Builders' Association, 20 Toronto St., Suite 400, Toronto, Ontario, Canada M5C 2B8. $6 US. Very thorough treatment.

E-448 _____. *Air Sealing Homes for Energy Conservation*. BETT Publication No. 84-2407/5. 1984. 350 pp. 580 Booth St., Ottawa, Canada K1A 0E4. A draft version. Detailed analysis and instructions.

E-450 _____. *Air Sealing Homes for Energy Conservation*. BETT Publication M-92-6/1984E. 460 O'Connor St., Ottawa, Ontario, Canada K1S 5H3. 1984. About 260 pp. Draft version. Excellent text and diagrams, but fails to mention specific brands.

G-340 Gofman, J. W., *Radiation and Human Health*. 1981. 910 pp. $30. Sierra Club Books, 530 Bush St., San Francisco CA 94108. Much detailed information.

L-50 Lenchek, Thomas, Chris Mattock, and John Raabe, *Superinsulated Design and Construction: a Guide to Building Energy-Efficient Homes*. 1987. 182 pp. $39.55. Van Nostrand Reinhold, 115 Fifth Ave., New York NY 10003. Available also from Northeast Solar Energy Association, PO Box 541, Brattleboro VT 05301, for $36.

L-200 Liddament, M. W., "Power Law Rules: OK?" *Air Infiltration Review*, Vol. 8, No. 2 (Feb. 1987), 4.

L-400 Lstiburek, J. W., and J. K. Lischkoff, *A New Approach to Affordable Low Energy House Construction*. Alberta (Canada) Department of Housing. July 1984. About 120 pp.

M-10 Marshall, Brian, and Robert Argue, *The Superinsulated Retrofit Book.* 1981. 208 pages. $12.95 Canadian. Renewable Energy in Canada, 107 Amelia St., Toronto, Ontario, Canada M4X 1E5. With clear text and excellent drawings and photographs, the authors explain in detail the many steps involved in the various methods of bringing old houses up to superinsulation standards.

M-76 Massachusetts Audubon Society, *Superinsulation: An Introduction To The Latest Energy Efficient Construction.* 36 pp. Free. Massachusetts Audubon Society, Lincoln MA 01773. An excellent summary, with first-rate drawings.

M-86 McAdams, W. H., *Heat Transmission,* 2nd ed. 1942. McGraw-Hill Book Co., New York NY. Famous basic text on heat flow; 45 years old but still one of the best.

M-92 McGrath, Edward, *How to Build a Superinsulated House.* 1978. 37 pp. $4. Privately published. Project 2020, Box 80707, College AK 99708. One of the very first books on superinsulation. Still helpful. Clear account of how to make houses snug even in an extremely cold climate.

M-93 _____. *A Working Guide for Owner-Builders, Architects, Carpenters and Contractors.* About 1981. 104 pp. $12. That New Publishing Co., 1525 Eielson St., Fairbanks AK 99707.

M-97 McRae, Alexander, Ed., *Energy Sourcebook.* 1977. Aspen Services Corp., Germantown MD.

N-25 National Academy of Sciences, Committee on Indoor Pollutants, *Indoor Pollutants.* Oct. 1981. 560 pp. $16.25. National Academy Press, 2101 Constitution Ave., Washington DC 20418. A mammoth, authoritative book.

N-200 Nazaroff, W. W. et al., "The Use of Mechanical Ventilation with Heat Recovery for Controlling Radon and Radon-Daughter Concentrations," LBL Report 10222. 1980. University of California at Berkeley.

N-700 Nisson, J. D. N., and Gautam Dutt, *The Superinsulated Home Book.* 1985. 330 pp. $34. John Wiley & Sons, 605 Third Ave., New York NY 10158. Also available from Northeast Solar Energy Association, PO Box 541, Brattleboro VT 05301. $34. The single best book on superinsulation building details. A must for architects, builders, and engineers.

O-145 Offerman, F. J., J. R. Girman, and C. D. Hollowell, "Midway House-Tightening Project: A study of Indoor Air Quality." LBL Report 12777. May 1981. 30 pp. University of California at Berkeley.

O-200 Orr, H. W., and R. S. Dumont: *A Major Energy Conservation Retrofit of a Bungalow.* 1984. Published by National Research Council, Division of Building Research, Saskatoon, Saskatchewan, Canada S7N 0W9.

S-145 Shapiro, A. M., *The Homeower's Complete Handbook for Add-on Solar Greenhouses and Sunspaces.* 1985. 360 pp. $12 paperback, $20 hardcover. Rodale Press, 33 East Minor St., Emmaus PA 18049. A big book containing a wealth of helpful information.

S-146 Shapiro, Jacob, *Radiation Protection.* 1981. 500 pp. Hardbound. $25. Published by the Harvard University Press, Cambridge, MA 02138. Much basic information on radon hazards.

S-162 Sheet Metal and Air Conditioning Contractors National Association, Inc., *Energy Recovery Equipment and Systems: Air-to-Air.* 1978. About 100 pp. $22.50. Published from 8224 Old Courthouse Rd., Tysons Corner, Vienna VA 22180.

S-185 Shick, W. A., R. A. Jones, W. S. Harris, and S. Konzo, *Technical Note 14: Details and Engineering Analysis of the Illinois Lo-Cal House.* May 1979. 110 pp. $8.50. Small Homes

Council, Building Research Council, University of Illinois, Urbana IL 61801. First detailed specifications of superinsulation. A classic.

S-240   Shurcliff, W. A., *Thermal Shutters and Shades*. 1980. 240 pp. $19.95. Brick House Publishing Co., PO Box 512, 3 Main St., Andover MA 01810. Describes more than 500 devices for reducing heat-loss through windows.

S-250   Shurcliff, W. A., *Super Solar Houses: Saunders' 100%-Solar Low-Cost Designs*. 140 pp. $12.95. Brick House Publishing Co., PO Box 512, 3 Main St., Andover MA 01810.

U-520-13   University of California, Lawrence Berkeley Laboratory, *Residential Ventilation with Heat Recovery: Improving Indoor Air Quality and Saving Energy*. (G. D. Roseme, J. V. Berk, et al.) Report LBL-9749. 1980. 29 pp.

PERIODICALS

Air infiltration Review, published by Air Infiltration and Ventilation Centre. Old Bracknell Lane West, Bracknell, Berkshire, Great Britain RG12 4AH. Summarizes all new information on infiltration and its control.

BETT Newsletter, published by Energy, Mines and Resources Canada, Building Energy Technology Transfer Program. Published from 580 Booth St., Ottawa, Canada K1A 0E4. Free. Presents news items, instructions on construction details, and lists of important BETT publications.

Custom Builder (formerly *Solar Age*; *Progressive Builder*), published by Solarvision, Inc., 120 Wilton Rd., Peterborough NH 03458. $24. Much information on insulation, infiltration, etc.

DNNA News, published by Fuller Moore, Dept of Architecture, Miami University, 125 Alumni Hall, Oxford OH 45056. A newsletter summarizing the latest methods of increasing the amount of daylight penetrating deep into buildings.

Home Energy (formerly *Energy Auditor and Retrofitter*), 2124 Kittredge, Suite 95, Berkeley CA 94704. Bimonthly. $25.

Energy Design Update, published by Cutter Information Corp., 1100 Massachusetts Ave., Arlington MA 02174. Edited by J. D. Ned Nisson, PO Box 1709, Ansonia Station, New York, NY 10023. Monthly. $85. Excellent news and comments on superinsulation materials and methods.

New England Builder, PO Box 278, Montpelier, VT 05602. $16. Tremendous coverage of all aspects of superinsulated house construction.

Practical Homeowner, published by Rodale Press, 33 East Minor St., Emmaus PA 18049. $13.

Index